Laura Stamm's
POWER SKATING

SECOND EDITION

LAURA STAMM

LEISURE PRESS
Champaign, Illinois

Developmental Editor: Sue Ingels Mauck
Copyeditor: David Dobbs
Assistant Editors: Robert King, Holly Gilly
Production Director: Ernie Noa
Typesetter: Yvonne Winsor
Text Design: Keith Blomberg
Text Layout: Denise Mueller, Denise Peters
Cover Design: Jack Davis
Cover Photo: Bruce Bennett
Interior Photos: Bruce Bennett, Jerry Liebman, Fran Doleszar
Interior Art: Gretchen Walters, Glenn Amundsen, Tim Offenstein
Printed By: Versa Press

796. 96
Sta
1989

On the Cover: Laura Stamm and Kevin Dineen

Photos of Herb Brooks and Bob Nystrom © Bruce Bennett, 35 Meadow Lane, Hicksville, NY 11801

ISBN: 0-88011-331-6

Copyright © 1989, 1982 by Laura Stamm

Library of Congress Cataloging-in-Publication Data

Stamm, Laura.
  [Power skating]
  Laura Stamm's power skating / Laura Stamm.—2nd ed.
    p. cm.
  Rev. ed. of: Power skating. ©1982.
  Bibliography: p.
  ISBN 0-88011-331-6
  1. Hockey—Training. 2. Skating. I. Stamm, Laura. Power
skating. II. Title. III. Title: Power skating.
GV848.3.S7 1989
796.96'2'07—dc19   88-12142
                                                           CIP

Printed in the United States of America

10 9 8 7 6 5

Leisure Press
A Division of Human Kinetics
  Publishers, Inc.
Box 5076, Champaign, IL
  61825-5076
1-800-747-4457

Europe Office:
Human Kinetics Publishers
  (Europe) Ltd.
P.O. Box IW14
Leeds LS16 6TR
England
0532-781708

Canada Office: ·
Human Kinetics Publishers, Inc.
P.O. Box 2503, Windsor, ON N8Y 4S2
1-800-465-7301 (in Canada only)

MAY 3 1993

To my beloved family—the cornerstone of my life.

To my extended family—all the hockey players, big and small, pro and peewee, from whom in the process of teaching I have learned and received so much.

And to all those who have believed in me and helped fulfill dreams beyond my imagination.

You all have enriched my life beyond measure and have showed me that there is no difference between learning and teaching.

CONTENTS

FOREWORDS

©Bruce Bennett

Anatoli Tarasov once said, "You will not get far using old skates, using old tactics, skill, and techniques." How right he was. Skating is the foundation for good hockey players and teams.

While there are different types and levels of skating ability, all players can improve through the use of skating techniques assisting them to be as competent as possible. Coaches should encourage players not to be afraid to look or feel funny in pursuit of good technique. Motivate them to operate at a high tempo after they have grasped the fundamentals of this book.

Hockey is the fastest game in the world. With her expertise Laura Stamm can help you lay the foundation to play it as fast as possible. I highly recommend this book for all coaches and players.

Herb Brooks
Coach, 1980 U.S. Gold Medal Olympic Team
Head Coach, New York Rangers, 1981-1985
Head Coach, Minnesota North Stars, 1987-1988

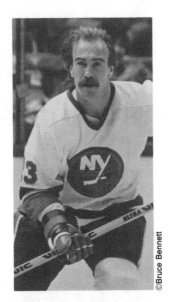

©Bruce Bennett

While playing junior hockey I was told that I would never make it to the National Hockey League because of my poor skating ability. As I look back now, that might well have come true if I hadn't taken power skating instruction from Laura Stamm. Laura's professional help started me off on the right foot toward what I felt was a fantastic 13-year career.

I improved my balance, speed, and agility on the ice after taking Laura's power skating clinics. During these clinics I was put through a variety of drills to help me understand the basics of skating. Whenever I had difficulty with my skating during the course of my career, I went back to doing those drills.

There is no substitute for the training and results that you can achieve from following the guidelines and drills in *Laura Stamm's Power Skating*. I recommend this book to anyone interested in playing hockey, whether you play just for recreation or are attempting to make it to the pros.

Bob Nystrom
Forward, New York Islanders, 1973-1986
Assistant Coach, New York Islanders, 1986-1988

PREFACE

Power skating is hockey skating; it covers the techniques for moving fast on ice while maintaining control at all times. It encompasses every aspect of skating necessary to develop into a more effective and valuable hockey player or pleasure skater, or both.

Skating remains the most neglected hockey skill. Time and again it is demonstrated that the best skaters become the most valuable players. Players have so much to think about in a game—stickhandling, shooting, passing, etc.—that they have little time to think about skating technique or how to react on skates to unexpected situations or sudden body checks. Players' skating ability must be honed so sharply that their reactions become second nature.

To most players, skating technique is the least exciting aspect of their hockey education. But concentration, experimentation, and dedication, not to mention practice and repetition, are necessary to develop explosive, agile skating and to change poor skating habits. In the end the attitude toward learning is pivotal, and often makes the difference between a champ and a chump.

Remember, hard work and progress are inseparable! The end result of all your efforts will be power with what I call *BAM-Balance, Agility,* and *Mobility.*

This book is a guide to help hockey players at all levels of ability from beginners to professionals. Some sections are, of course, more suited to developing players: Chapters 1 through 4 cover coaching tips, skates, and equipment and the basics of how skate blades function. Other chapters are more complex, from forward and backward strides (chapters 5 and 6) to turns and agility exercises (chapters 10 and 11). Drills begin with the simpler exercises and become progressively more difficult. The advanced sections will be of special interest to highly skilled players who desire a more intensive study of skating and still greater perfection of their skills. The final chapter provides an overview of training and conditioning techniques for developing an all-inclusive hockey program. The glossary is a useful tool for putting this book to work for you.

Although the book is divided into chapters related to various facets of skating, many of these areas merge into and rely upon one another. To perform one skating technique well—starting, for example—often requires that the student be able to execute other maneuvers well, such as stopping, balancing, and edge control. Therefore, improving your skating requires an all encompassing program, just as a proper diet includes all the required nutrients. There are no exceptions, and no player is excluded: Goalies should skate and perform all maneuvers and exercises with the rest of the team.

Goalies often believe that they are excused from skating because they're "only standing in front of the net." However, goalies' reflexes and performances depend on balance, agility, and strength on skates. Their goals against average often improves dramatically as their skating improves.

The drills in this book should be done first without a puck and then, as your mastery improves, with a puck, to integrate skating moves with stickhandling skills. No instant method for becoming a successful skater exists. Results depend upon your degree of input. Development entails experimentation, trial and error, and plenty of falls. Mistakes are inevitable. The rewards for diligence, however, are worth the effort both for the player and the team. A better skater will score more goals, stop the opposition from scoring, and help the team win games.

So have fun, work hard, and SKATE, SKATE, SKATE!

ACKNOWLEDGMENTS

Books often have just one author, but most could never be written without the help of many. I express deep thanks and gratitude to all who helped make this book a reality:

The Hartford Whalers and Emile Francis, general manager, for their assistance and cooperation.

NHL players Doug Brown, Kevin Dineen, and Keith Gretzky for their time, patience, and great skating.

Herb Brooks, with whom I had the honor of working when he coached the New York Rangers, and Bob Nystrom, assistant coach of the New York Islanders, for their encouragement and support of my Power Skating System.

Jack Blatherwick, exercise physiologist and conditioning specialist for the New York Rangers (1985-87) and for the U.S. Olympic hockey teams of 1980, 1984, and 1988, for his technical assistance in developing the chapter on training and conditioning. His expertise was invaluable.

Marshall Rule, for his knowledge and technical advice, as well as for the intellectual battles that still serve to further my education in skating.

Hal Walsh, for his expert critiquing of the book. His analyses were instrumental in improving the content and quality.

The Darien Ice Rink in Darien, Connecticut, and Doug Scott, manager, for their cooperation and assistance.

All the hockey players who contributed their time, energy and skating in the making of this book: Todd Brost, Gordon Campbell, Glen Cucinell, Mark Pecchia, Bryant Perrier, Louis Santini, Craig Speed, and Richard Stamm.

The following equipment companies and organizations for their support and assistance: Cooper International, Itech, Micron Skates, Okanagan Hockey School (Penticton, British Columbia), Rollerblades Training Skates, and Titan Hockey Sticks.

Photographers Bruce Bennett, Fran Doleszar, and Jerry Liebman and illustrators Mark Pickrell, Tim Offenstein, Gretchen Walters, and Glenn Amundsen for their time and great work.

Sue Mauck, my editor at Leisure Press, who tirelessly (thank goodness) pushed me to produce a book far better than would have been possible had I been deprived of her infinite patience and meticulous attention to detail.

The King Salmon Lodge, King Salmon, Alaska, for extending to me a haven of peace and beauty that provided the atmosphere to accomplish this difficult and often tedious task.

Chapter

1

COACHES' CORNER

Every hockey coach wants his or her players to develop their hockey and skating skills to their best ability. But as knowledgeable as a coach may be about offensive, defensive, and strategic aspects of the game, he or she may not be well versed in the science of power skating.

Imagine the frustration of a hockey coach who sees players skating ineffectively but who can't pinpoint how to correct their errors. Skating, after all, is a highly specialized science. Increasing numbers of coaches are studying power skating techniques or employing power skating specialists to train players in this vital aspect of the sport.

Obviously skating is not the most exciting aspect of hockey training. Kids want to play the game—not practice skating. The challenge for a coach or power skating instructor is first to teach skating principles so they are well understood, and then to design exercises that are stimulating, functional, and offer enough variety so that learning and practice don't become tedious. Once players realize that their hockey is improving because their skating is improving they'll be willing students. After all, hockey is more fun to play when you skate well.

People learn in different ways. Some learn visually, some learn by imitating, others learn by feeling, and yet others learn as a result of understanding. No single method works for everyone. Usually the learning process requires a combination of approaches. In teaching a group, coaches must use all methods in combination so that all students can benefit. In teaching an individual, coaches must discover the learning modes that work best for that person and adhere to them. Feel out what works and what doesn't work. Change your words and images accordingly. Some students do better when left on their own to work out ideas. Others need gentle prodding. Some need downright insistence. All need encouragement.

I have found that for me, teaching by saying "Follow me" or "Do this" doesn't work. Players may try to "do this," but 20 people see 20 different things and although they *think* they are "doing this" they are actually doing something quite different. I have also discovered that asking "Do you understand?" is inadequate. Very few players have the courage to admit that they don't understand. They'll act as if they do, then perform incorrectly. Test their comprehension verbally and by performance. Encourage them to communicate their uncertainties and to ask questions. Help the players to find their own answers by asking them questions. The result will be a tangible and enduring education.

My favorite expressions follow:

- *Feel* what you're doing
- *Act* out what you feel
- *See* (visualize) how the move should look
- *Think* (analyze) why
- **F**eel, **A**ct, **S**ee, **T**hink = **FAST**

Tips for Coaches of Young Players

1. We are teachers and should approach coaching with that in mind. Our job is to stimulate the enjoyment of learning, the inquisitiveness and creativity of young people, and their love for the sport.
2. Learn from watching the best. I study players like Paul Coffey, Dennis Savard, and Glen Anderson by videotaping their rushes and watching each maneuver in slow motion.
3. Provide incentives to learning and improving. Reward is far more effective than punishment.
4. Although each individual's skating movement is unique, certain universal skating principles must be adhered to if one is to reach an optimum potential. It is the coach's job to teach those principles and design fun exercises to implement and practice them.
5. It takes years to develop a finished skater. Don't expect instant success.

6. Make learning fun. Since youngsters easily get restless, try to keep them skating as much as possible rather than having them stand around awaiting their turn to skate. Organize exercises with this in mind. To avoid crowding, skate the entire length of ice when the group is small, but skate from sideboards to sideboards when the group is large. Also, try to sense when the group grows restless and change the drills immediately.

7. Use prizes and races to stimulate the competitive spirit. Note, however, that races can be helpful once skills have been developed, but can be detrimental when skills are just being learned. Players caught in the frenzy of trying to win forget about technique.

8. When possible, divide players into skating lines and explain the exercises of the day and their purposes before going on the ice. Players will then understand your goals for the practice and be ready to work when they hit the ice. Since ice time has a way of flying by, the less talk and the more skating time the better.

9. Respect begets respect. Use praise when it is deserved and treat all players with dignity. Coaches do not have to rule by intimidation.

10. Reassure players that mistakes are not high crimes. Many fear looking bad and refuse to experiment for fear of embarrassment, criticism, or even reprimand. Negative feedback decreases the willingness to take risks, so keep reminding them that everyone, even the pros, fall, and that in learning, mistakes are inevitable and are often simply an indication that the player is trying something new. Not only should the coach accept mistakes, he or she should acknowledge a good try even when a player wipes out. The improvement once players no longer fear criticism is amazing to behold. You might even take a dive yourself once in a while. It shows that nobody, even the teacher, is perfect.

11. Rely on players who take learning seriously. More often than not, they turn out to be your most reliable performers.

Using the Exercises

The exercises in this book are flexible enough to be used in all kinds of combinations, and they are interchangeable with one another. For example, coaches may:

1. Combine turn exercises with knee-drop exercises.

2. Combine crossover exercises with pivots.
3. Use obstacle courses.
4. Use a stopwatch to time the players.

POINTS TO REMEMBER

- Develop a philosophy of teaching and adhere to it.
- Affection and discipline are not mutually exclusive.
- Teaching can sometimes be like pulling teeth, but insistence on high standards pays off. Whenever possible, learning should be fun, but sometimes players must be made to learn in spite of themselves.
- Inventiveness, creativity, and analytic thinking should be encouraged. Too many youngsters have their individuality and creativity stifled by the time they're 10 by screaming coaches. A Wayne Gretzky is not the product of fear but of the freedom to *Feel, Act, See,* and *Think* (FAST) and make mistakes along the way.
- Keep learning. There is no difference between learning and teaching!

Chapter

2

SKATES AND EQUIPMENT

A bargain pair of skates invariably turns out to be a bad investment. And buying boots a few sizes too large so that a youngster can use them for a few years is penny-wise and pound-foolish. To skate well, a skater must have well-constructed skates that fit correctly.

Buying and Fitting Skates

The function of the skate boots is to support the feet firmly so that the skater can execute the necessary maneuvers (see Figure 2.1). Good boots feature a counter (instep) made of reinforcing material, which makes that area of the boots supportive for the arches and ankles. When a skater's ankles cave in, the cause is usually not weak ankles but poorly fitted skates or skates with poorly designed counters. Lack of ankle support virtually guarantees that skating will be unpleasant because of the pain from caved-in ankles. Weak ankles are generally a myth, unless there has been a specific injury to the foot. Skates that fit properly can improve performance enormously. Those that don't fit properly almost guarantee difficulties.

In today's market players can choose from a range of high quality skates, either leather, molded plastic, or a combination of both. All high quality skates offer high-level performance. Some last longer than others, and some offer better protection against injury from pucks or sticks. No matter which type of skate you choose, make

Figure 2.1   Typical hockey skate.

sure they fit well and are laced properly. Then you will be prepared to use your skates to develop speed, agility, and power.

Follow these guidelines for selecting skates:

1. Boots must fit snugly, though the toes should not be pinched. They should hug the feet firmly, leaving a little toe space at the front. Your heels should not move up and down in the boots.
2. Wear the same weight of sock when fitting your new boots as you will wear when skating. A sock of different weight can change the size and fit. A thin sock is best so that the boots can mold themselves to the feet during the months ahead.
3. Unlace the boots most of the way before putting them on. Trying to jam your foot into a boot that is three-quarters laced will make it seem as if the boot is too tight.
4. Make sure the boots are of proper width. When the skates are laced there should be a spread of 1½ to 2 inches between the eyelets on the same row. The boots should fit snugly at the instep and across the ball of the foot. If the skates are too wide, your ankles will cave in when skating. If the skates are too long, your heels will lift up when you lean forward. And if the heels are not snug, you may get blisters.
5. Your skate boot size is not necessarily the same as your shoe size. Many skate boots are sized differently from street shoes.

Also, each brand is cut differently, so one brand might fit you well while another may be uncomfortable.

6. When buying skates, go to a shop specializing in skates and hockey equipment. It is important to be fitted by someone who knows skates.

Lacing the Skates

Although at first it may not seem critical, lacing one's skates properly is essential to good performance. Unfortunately, many skaters overtighten their laces; this limits foot mobility. Boots should support the feet, not act as casts and inhibit good skating. Good lacing will firmly support your feet while allowing you to comfortably roll your ankles and boots inward and outward without restriction. Boots laced too tightly may cut into your flesh and restrict your ability to roll your ankles.

The toe area and the area high above the ankles should be laced so they are moderately snug or even on the loose side. Some players choose not to lace the top eyelets. The tightest area of lacing should be from a point above the ball of the foot back to a point just above the ankle bone. This is where the most support is required (Figure 2.2). If laces are too tight at the top, bending your knees

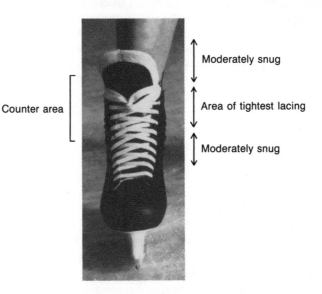

Figure 2.2   Correct lacing of the boot.

and ankles becomes difficult. In addition, circulation to the feet may be cut off, causing numbness and foot cramps. Don't pull your laces so tight that you're in pain! Also, there is no need to wrap tape around your ankles. This inhibits the foot mobility needed for edging. If you must use tape, wrap it loosely and use it sparingly.

The Skate Blades

First-rate hockey skates require blades of high quality, heat-tempered steel that will retain a sharp edge despite extremely rough use. Avoid wearing your blades anywhere except on the ice or on the rubber mats provided by rinks in the locker rooms and walk-ways. Walking on hard floors nicks and dulls your blades. Inexpensive blades are a poor investment because they nick and dull easily, and thus have to be sharpened frequently. Most high quality boots have high quality blades, but there are several brands of blades. Players often buy the blades of their choice and have them put on their boots.

Blade Design

Each skate blade, from toe to heel, is designed with two knifelike edges separated by a groove in between. The function of the groove is to expose the edges, enabling them to cut into the ice more effectively. This groove is called the hollow (Figure 2.3). The skate can be sharpened so that the hollow is either shallow or deep, depending on the player's preference. In general, too much hollow makes

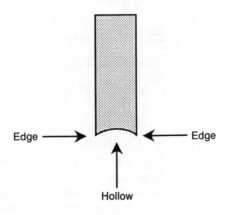

Edge ⟶   ⟵ Edge

Hollow

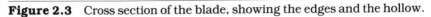

Figure 2.3   Cross section of the blade, showing the edges and the hollow.

it difficult to execute a smooth, effective stop, because the edges can unexpectedly dig into the ice, causing a sudden fall. Too little hollow makes it difficult to execute sharp turns and powerful pushes.

Children require sharp blades and a relatively deep hollow so that the edges will cut into the ice more easily, since there is little body weight to press down against the surface. Conversely, heavier people can skate with a shallower hollow.

The bottom of hockey skate blades are convex (curved) in shape. This curved shape is called the *rock*, or radius, and is similar in shape to a crescent moon (Figure 2.4). The rock of the blade makes it possible for skaters to maneuver in tight curves and circles. If the blades were straight like those of speed skates, hockey players could gain speed when skating straight ahead but it would be difficult to weave, cut, or execute sharp turns. Goalies, by contrast, wear blades that are almost straight on the bottom rather than convex, because goalies need to quickly move straight ahead, backward, or sideways rather than perform weaving or circular maneuvers. Curved blades would also hinder their ability to make skate saves. Goaltenders don't sharpen their skates as often as other players do, since duller blades allow them to slide sideways across the goal crease.

Figure 2.4   Hockey blade, showing the rock.

If a blade is sharpened and *rockered* (curved) to an extreme degree, very little of the blade's length makes contact with the ice. Heavily rockered skate blades are popular with some pros, which encourages many young skaters to rock their blades also. This is unfortunate since it can cause balance problems and restrict power and speed because so little blade engages the ice.

Sharpening the Blades

Blades should be kept sharp and free from nicks and dents. Dull, nicked blades do not grip the ice effectively when pressure is applied; the result is a loss of power, speed, and maneuverability. Dull blades can unexpectedly slip out from under the skater. If this happens during a sudden move, it can cause painful muscle pulls or tears and unexpected falls.

Blades should be sharpened when you feel they are no longer cutting crisply into the ice. They should be sharpened by an expert. Some professional hockey players sharpen their skates after every game; some even do it after each period. However, this isn't necessary or even desirable for most nonprofessional players, as excessive sharpening shortens the life of the blades.

How to Test the Sharpening

A properly sharpened blade's edges are level with each other. To test the accuracy of the sharpening, place a coin horizontally on the upturned blade. Study the angle of the coin. If it is perfectly level, the edges are even (Figure 2.5). If the coin leans to either side, take the skates back for resharpening; if one edge is higher than the other, your skating will be impaired.

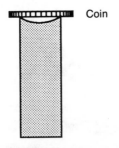 Coin

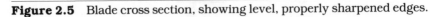

Figure 2.5   Blade cross section, showing level, properly sharpened edges.

If the sharpener is not careful, blades may become increasingly rockered with successive sharpenings, leaving too little blade in contact with the ice. Don't allow this to happen. Tell the sharpener precisely how sharp you want them, how much hollow you want, and how much rock you want. Draw a template by tracing the outline of your blades' arcs after they are first sharpened. After each successive sharpening, make sure that the rock conforms to that outline. Also, ask the sharpener to hand stone the blades after each sharpening. This ensures smooth, finished edges.

How Blade Edges Function

The blade edges at the inner sides of the boots are called the inside edges (Figure 2.6a), and those on the outer sides are called the outside edges (Figure 2.6b). The edges have a specific purpose: to cut into the ice. In doing this they perform two different functions, pushing and gliding.

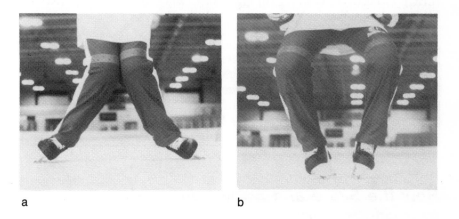

a   b

Figure 2.6   (a) Inside and (b) outside edges.

Pushing

Proper use of skate blade edges is the secret of stability and power on ice. The blade edge digging into the ice provides the grip against which the leg must thrust for power and speed. If you try to push without using the edge to first dig into the ice, your skate will slip. You may attribute this to the ice being slippery. The ice should never feel slippery. If you use your edges properly, you will always have a good grip on the ice. You should feel that you are cutting the ice with the edges. Even when gliding straight ahead on two feet, you should incline slightly toward the inside edges for grip and stability.

Gliding

The blade edge, when used for gliding, determines the direction of travel. Because the blade is rockered, an engaged edge travels a curved path. When gliding on the left forward inside edge (LFI), for instance, you will move in a clockwise direction. Gliding on the right forward inside edge (RFI), you will move in a counterclockwise direction. Gliding on the left forward outside edge (LFO) you move in a counterclockwise direction, and gliding on the right forward outside edge (RFO), you move in a clockwise direction.

Going backward, the directions are reversed. Gliding on left backward inside edge (LBI): counterclockwise. Gliding on right backward inside edge (RBI): clockwise. Gliding on left backward outside edge (LBO): clockwise. Gliding on right backward outside edge (RBO): counterclockwise.

Glide direction	Edge
Clockwise	LFI, RFO, RBI, LBO
Counterclockwise	RFI, LFO, LBI, RBO

How the Skate and Body Coordinate to Produce Curves

A common misconception in hockey is that your skates should always be held straight up. When your skates are held straight up you ride simultaneously on the inside and outside edges (the flats) of the blades. Since the flat of the blade describes a straight line on the ice, you will glide either straight forward or straight back. You cannot glide on a curve, however, nor can you grip the ice, with the flat of the blade. You must use the edges.

To get an edge to cut into the ice, you must lean the engaged boot so that the edge forms a sharper angle with the ice. This is done by pressing the engaged foot (the pushing or gliding foot) onto its side—it can be either the outside or the inside—and bending that knee. Two important points:

1. When the thrusting (pushing) foot is on an edge, the more your foot presses, your boot leans, and your knee bends, the more the skate will grip the ice and the greater the potential for thrust

against the ice. An edge that wedges into the ice at an angle of 45 degrees is the optimum cutting edge. Try to achieve a knee bend of 90 degrees, measured from thigh to shin on the pushing leg (Figure 2.7).

Figure 2.7   Thrusting foot on an edge.

2. When your gliding foot (skating foot) is on an edge, the more your foot presses, your boot leans, and your knee bends, the sharper will be your curve or circle. Try to achieve a knee bend of 90 degrees on the gliding leg.

The skate alone cannot achieve the edge. Your entire body must work to produce an effective pushing or gliding edge. If you want to apply the inside edge, lean your boot, knee, and thigh toward the inside of your body (Figure 2.8a). If you want to apply the outside edge, lean your boot, knee, and thigh toward the outside of your body. (Figure 2.8b). The angle of your knee and thigh must line up above the skate so that all describe the same angle to the ice. The rest of your body weight (hips, torso, shoulders) presses downward toward the ice to assist the edge in gripping the ice. If your body weight pulls up away from the ice the edge will grip less effectively and the curve will be shallow.

There are special factors involved in skating on a curve or circle:

1. The faster you travel, the deeper an edge you can apply to the ice.
2. Centripetal and centrifugal forces are at work; they must be

a   b

Figure 2.8   (a) Gliding forward on inside edge (left foot); (b) gliding forward on outside edge (left foot).

equalized and in proportion to your speed so that you can balance.

3. The skate blade travels as if it were on the outside rim of a circle. Your body rides slightly inside the rim. The lower body (skating foot, knee, thigh, and hips) presses toward the center of the circle. Your hips should face the line of travel. The upper body (chest and shoulder) rests above your hips but still within the rim of the circle. If your upper body presses into the

Figure 2.9   Body position for skating a curve.

circle more than your lower body does, your stability will be jeopardized.

4. Figure 2.9 shows the body position essential to effective movement on a curve. Expert hockey players frequently employ this position for difficult maneuvers such as tight turns, crossovers, or pivots.

Coaches often tell skaters to lean into the circle to obtain their curve. However, this advice often leads to the misconception that the upper body should be tilted into the circle. Only the skate, knee, thigh, and hip should lean into the circle. The upper body should be essentially upright. Figure 2.10 illustrates the undesirable results of tilting the upper body. Correct body positioning is one of the most

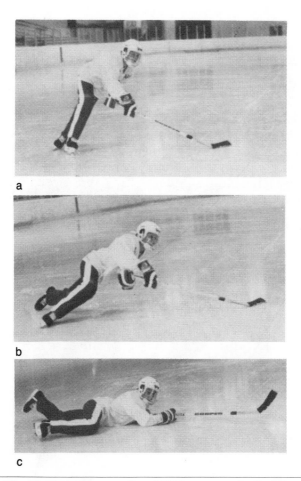

a

b

c

Figure 2.10 Undesirable results of tilting upper body into curve.

important aspects of balance and must be mastered to become a good hockey skater.

Protective Equipment

When performing the exercises in this book, always wear well-designed protective hockey gear: helmet, gloves, elbow pads, shin guards, and shoulder guards. Because the exercises require experimentation, falls are inevitable and should be considered as normal as breathing. By wearing your equipment when practicing, you lower the risk of injury and become accustomed to skating at your game weight (Figures 2.11a and b).

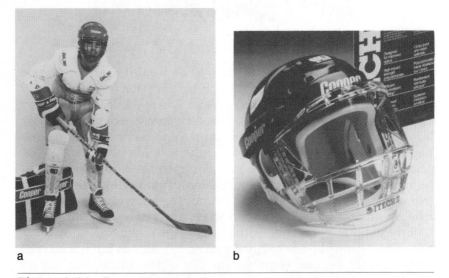

a   b

Figure 2.11 Protective equipment.

3

BALANCE

Balance is the proper distribution of body weight over the skates. It is an often elusive but always important skill that is acquired only after months or even years of practice. When you have mastered it you will enjoy greater maneuverability and speed, but until you do, your control and speed will be limited and other hockey players may easily knock you down.

Strive for such fine balance that you give the impression of being linked to the ice by a magnetic force. Mastering balance will give you the ability to withstand crunching body checks and high velocity turns as well as sudden stops and changes of direction.

Many different balance situations exist, and all should be mastered. Some players balance well on two skates but not on one. Some balance on one skate on the flat of the blade, but not on an edge. Some maneuver adequately when skating forward but not when skating backward. Others balance well when skating slowly but not rapidly, or vice versa, or are competent when skating counterclockwise but flounder when attempting clockwise curves. Still others skate well while icebound but if they have to jump into the air have trouble recovering their balance or stride on landing.

Lack of balance when skating backward is a common and often serious weakness. All players, not only those playing defense, should strive to improve their balance on all backward skating moves. This will make them more versatile in game situations.

Balance is largely controlled by upper body positioning and by weight distribution over the skates. Proper development and use of the back muscles is critical. While the legs are the "engines" and are used for power and motion, the job of the back muscles is to hold the upper body still, or balanced, above the moving skates.

Goalies need superb balance. Goalies often must fall to the ice to make saves, then return to their feet quickly. Good balance is necessary for these fast recoveries (Figures 3.1a and b). Making a kick save without falling also requires excellent balance. Too often goalies go down not because they want to but because they can't stay on their feet. When that happens they are at the mercy of the opposition.

a   b

Figure 3.1   Balance and quick recovery as needed by goalies.

Balance on Two Skates

Balance on two skates is important when a player is gliding slowly—for example, when waiting for a pass or for a play to develop. It is also important when checking or being checked by an opponent. The following paragraphs explain how to balance on the flats and edges of the blades of both skates.

Balance on the Flats of the Blades (Skating Forward)

1. The proper stance when gliding forward on the flats of both blades is with your feet held about shoulder width apart, knees bent. In this position you are stable and prepared to thrust off (see chapter 5, "The Forward Stride," for explanation).

2. Your shoulders should be held back. Concentrate on maintaining a vertical position by using your back muscles and keeping your head up. Slumping or looking down will result in a loss of balance by causing your body weight to pitch over the curved toes of the blades. Holding the upper body still is also critical to balance and control in skating.
3. Keep your body weight on the back halves (from the middle to the heels) of the blades.
4. Keep the skate blades in full contact with the ice. Figure 3.2 illustrates proper balance; Figures 3.3a, b, and c are examples of what not to do: Never lean on your stick for balance or support.

Figure 3.2   Proper balance.

a   b   c

Figure 3.3   (a and b) Results of poor balance and (c) leaning on stick.

Balance on the Flats of the Blades (Skating Backward)

The rules for forward balance on two skates apply also to backward balance, except that your body weight must be maintained farther forward on the blades—on the front halves of the blades, but *not* on the curved toes. If your weight is over your toes you may pitch over the fronts of your skates. If your weight is over your heels you may fall over backward.

Balance on the Inside Edges

When gliding slowly forward or backward to wait for a play or pass, you should be in a balance stance with your feet wider apart than your shoulders, both skates on their inside edges, knees flexed (Figure 3.4). Even minimal use of the inside edges provides more stability than using the flats of the skates. This stance gives you excellent stability. You are prepared to move laterally, straight ahead, or straight back. All you need to do to move is shift your weight onto the pushing foot and thrust off. The more you dig in the inside edges and bend your knees, the more traction you will get, and the harder you will be to knock down. If you are about to be checked and do not have time to do anything else, you can widen your stance, dig in the inside edges, and bend your knees, increasing your stability.

Goalies almost always stand on the inside edges. Good balance on the inside edges and a knowledge of how to use them are extremely important when guarding the net.

Figure 3.4   Gliding in wide stance on inside edges.

Balance on One Skate

Balance on one skate should be mastered skating both forward and backward, first on the flat of the blade and then on the inside and outside edges. You never know when you will be startled with a body check while on only one skate—for example, following a hard jolt, or when you must lunge, jump, evade, or leap over another player and land on one foot. You will not be a proficient player until you can be perfectly comfortable moving on one skate, either forward or backward, on the flat or on either edge.

Balance on the Flat of the Blade

Balancing on the flat of the blade can be compared to balancing on a tightrope; all your weight must be directly over the gliding or skating foot, with the full blade in contact with the ice. Place your weight solidly over the gliding foot so the skate cannot wiggle or move around (Figure 3.5). Keep your hips facing straight ahead. If you lean to either side, forward, or back, you may lose your footing (Figure 3.6).

Posture is critical to balance. Your shoulders must be held back, your back held straight. Keep head and chin up. When your shoulders slump forward or you look down, your weight pitches over the curved toe of the blade and you may lose your balance.

Figure 3.5   Proper balance on flat of the blade.

Figure 3.6   Poor balance.

Balance on the Inside of the Blade (Skating Forward)

Balancing on the inside edge is more difficult than balancing on the flat. However, it is essential to do so, because players glide on, shoot, check, and thrust from inside edges.

When you are told to lean your boot onto its side so the edge forms a 45-degree angle to the ice and then to stand on the edge in that position, your initial reaction will probably be that you won't be able to. This may be true at first. But eventually, after practice, you will be able to balance well on a single edge. You will in fact find it not only possible, but a vital prerequisite to skating effectively.

Figure 3.7   Skating forward on left inside edge.

To skate and balance on the inside edge of your left foot (LFI), lean your left skate, knee, and thigh strongly toward the center of your body so the inside blade edge cuts into the ice at a strong angle (an effective angle at high speeds is 45 degrees). Using your right foot as the pushing foot, thrust off and glide forward on the left inside edge. Lift your right foot off the ice after you thrust and hold it close to the skating foot as you glide on the inside edge (Figure 3.7). Keep your skating (left) knee well bent, your body weight on the back half of the blade, and your hips facing your line of travel. You will curve in a clockwise direction. Remember: The more you lean your skate, knee, and thigh, the smaller the circle.

To do this on your right foot (RFI), mirror the above procedure. You will curve in a counterclockwise direction.

Balance on the Outside Edge of the Blade (Skating Forward)

Balancing on the outside edge is initially more difficult than balancing on either the flat or the inside edge. Regardless of difficulty, it is an essential aspect of skating on a curve.

To skate and balance on the outside edge of your left foot (LFO), lean your left skate, knee, and thigh strongly toward the outside (left) of your body so the outside blade edge cuts into the ice at a strong angle, about 45 degrees. Using your right foot as the pushing foot, thrust off and glide forward on the left outside edge. Lift your right foot off the ice after you thrust and hold it close to the skating foot as you glide on the outside edge (Figure 3.8). Keep your

Figure 3.8 Skating forward on left outside edge.

skating knee well bent and your body weight on the back half of the blade. You will be skating in a counterclockwise direction.

To do this on the right foot (RFO), mirror the above procedure. You will curve in a clockwise direction.

Balance on the Inside and Outside Edges (Skating Backward)

Hockey players must be able to skate and balance on one edge as effectively during backward moves as when skating forward. To balance while skating backward on one skate on an inside or outside edge, the procedure is essentially the same as for forward skating, with two major differences:

1. Your weight should be on the front half of the blade rather than on the back half.
2. The direction of curve produced by gliding on each edge is opposite from that produced by forward edges. See the section on edges in chapter 2 for the directions the edges travel.

NOTE: When skating a curve, keep your shoulders level. Beware of the common error of dropping the inside shoulder into the circle. Doing this leans too much body weight into the circle, resulting in a loss of balance. When in doubt, keep the inside shoulder slightly higher than the outside shoulder.

Combining Balance Exercises With Warm-Up Exercises

Many balance exercises are also useful as warm-up exercises. When used this way they should be done as the first exercises of the day.

When balance exercises are part of your warm-up, the order in which they are performed is important. Muscles require a chance to warm up gradually. If ice time is limited, warm-ups can be done off the ice, but they then serve only as warm-up exercises and do not help to develop better balance on the ice. Do them on the ice when possible.

Don't take balance for granted. The exercises in this chapter will improve balance, but good balance cannot be maintained without constant practice and attention. Balance is one of the first skills to be affected by even a brief layoff.

Unless specified otherwise, all exercises in this section should be executed while skating backward as well as forward. Perform them in the order they are presented to allow for gradual warming of the muscles.

Balance on the Flat of the Blade on One Skate (Thigh Muscle Warm-Up)

Skate from the goal line to the blue line. At the blue line raise your right knee as high as possible toward the stick, which should be held horizontally at arm's length at shoulder height, and glide on your left skate on the flat of the blade (see Figure 3.9). Try to glide to the opposite goal line before putting your right foot down. Repeat the exercise, lifting your left knee and gliding on your right skate. Raising the knee of your free leg gradually loosens the thigh muscles.

Many skaters are able to balance better on one foot than on the other. Give extra attention to your weaker foot to equalize right and left sides.

Figure 3.9   Balance on the flat of the blade—thigh muscle warm-up.

Balance on the Inside Edge on One Skate (Thigh Muscle Warm-Up)

1. Skate forward on the RFI. Raise your left knee up toward the stick, which is held horizontally, chest high. See how long you

can glide on the RFI before putting your right foot down. You will curve in a counterclockwise direction (see Figure 3.10).

2. Reverse the exercise, skating forward on the LFI in a clockwise direction.

3. Repeat steps 1 and 2, this time skating backward on the RBI and then on the LBI. You will travel a clockwise curve when skating on the RBI; when skating on the LBI you will travel a counterclockwise curve.

4. Skate a complete circle on the RFI, and then on the LFI. Remember: The lean into the circle comes from your skating foot, knee, and thigh. If your upper body (chest and shoulders) leans into the circle, you will have too much weight pitching into the circle and you will lose your balance.

5. Skate a complete circle on the RBI, and then on the LBI.

Figure 3.10 Balance on the inside edge—thigh muscle warm-up.

Balance on the Outside Edge on One Skate (Thigh Muscle Warm-Up)

1. Skate forward on the LFO. Raise your right knee up to the stick, which is held horizontally, chest high. See how long you can glide on the LFO before putting your right foot down. You will curve in a counterclockwise direction (see Figure 3.11).

2. Reverse the exercise, skating forward on the RFO in a clockwise direction.

3. Do the same skating backward on the LBO, and then on the RBO. When skating on the LBO you will travel a clockwise

curve; you will travel counterclockwise when skating on the RBO.

4. Skate a complete circle on the LFO and then on the RFO. Remember: The lean into the circle comes from your skating foot, knee, and thigh. Your upper body (chest and shoulders) must not tilt into the circle. If it does, you will be off balance.

5. Repeat, skating backward on the LBO, then on the RBO.

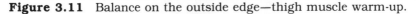

Figure 3.11   Balance on the outside edge—thigh muscle warm-up.

Balance on the Flats of the Blades on Two Feet (Hamstring Stretch)

Glide forward on both skates, feet shoulder width apart. Hold the hockey stick horizontally above your head. Then bend down and

Figure 3.12   Hamstring stretch.

reach toward your toes with the stick, keeping your knees straight and your weight on the back halves of the blades (Figure 3.12). Do the same exercise moving backward, with your weight now on the front halves of the blades. Always keep the entire blade lengths in contact with the ice. If your heels come off the ice, you may fall forward over your toes. Hold the stretch for approximately 10 seconds. *Do not bounce*: Bouncing can cause muscle pulls.

Twists

Glide on both skates, feet about shoulder width apart. Hold the hockey stick behind your neck with a hand on each end of the stick, and twist your arms from side to side (Figure 3.13). While twisting, reach your right elbow toward your left hip. Hold the stretch, then reach your left elbow toward your right hip. This loosens neck, back, and waist muscles.

Figure 3.13   Twist to loosen neck, back, and waist muscles.

Groin Stretch

This exercise can be done skating backward, but it is quite difficult to do. It is generally done skating forward.

This exercise must be done gently at first and gradually intensified. Since groin muscles are prone to injury they must be thoroughly warmed up before hard skating or beginning a game. The exercise is also excellent for improving balance and knee bend.

Glide on your right skate, on the flat of the blade. Bend your right knee as much as possible so that your buttocks are close to the ice and stretch your left leg behind you, keeping it on the ice with the foot in a turned-out position (Figure 3.14). Keep your shoulders back, back straight, and head up. Your stick should be held in one hand and kept on the ice in front of you. Your weight must be on the back half of your gliding foot. Do not lean forward.

Repeat the exercise, alternating legs. Gradually stretch your extended leg farther back as your groin muscles loosen. Do not bounce.

Figure 3.14   Groin stretch.

Forward Swizzles

This exercise is done with both skates on the ice and with the legs moving simultaneously. It is a good exercise for loosening the groin and inside thigh muscles (adductors) as well as for improving balance on inside edges.

Start with your feet in a V position, heels together, toes apart, on the inside edges of both skates. Bend your knees, keeping your weight on the back halves of the blades (Figure 3.15a). Move the toes of both skates as far apart as possible as you move forward. As your toes separate, straighten your knees (Figure 3.15b). Then turn your toes inward and slowly pull them together, keeping your knees straight (Figure 3.15c). Your toes will touch, forming an inverted V (Figure 3.15d). Form the original V and repeat the maneuver.

a

b

c

d

Figure 3.15 Forward swizzles.

Backward Swizzles

This procedure is the reverse of the forward swizzles. Start with your feet in an inverted V position, toes touching, heels apart, on the inside edges. Bend your knees, keeping your weight on the front halves of the blades. Pull your heels as far apart as possible as you move backward. As your heels separate, straighten your knees. Then draw your heels together to form the letter V. After your heels touch, bring your toes together again to form the original inverted V, and repeat the maneuver.

Leg Lifts

NOTE: Leg lifts must be done gently at first to gradually loosen the hamstring, quadricep, groin, and gluteal muscles.

1. Glide on your left skate, holding the hockey stick in front of you, horizontally, at shoulder height. See how long you can glide while keeping your right leg raised straight out in front of you and parallel to the ice. Do the same gliding on your right skate and lifting your left leg. Beginners should glide on the flat of the blade (Figure 3.16a), while more advanced skaters can glide on the edges for a more difficult test of balance.
2. Glide on your left skate, on the flat of the blade. Hold the stick horizontally in front of you at shoulder height. Balancing on your left skate, lift your right leg up and try to reach the stick (Figure 3.16b). Repeat, balancing on your right skate and lifting your left leg.
3. Glide on the flat of your left skate. Still holding your stick horizontally in front of you at shoulder height, lift your right leg up to the stick in front of you (Figure 3.16b), then out to the side (Figure 3.16c), and then behind you (Figure 3.16d). During these leg lifts keep the free leg as straight as possible for optimum stretching of the hamstring, thigh, groin, and gluteal muscles. Lift as high as possible and do not let the free leg touch the ice between lifts. *Do not kick*! Repeat, lifting the left leg.

a   b   (cont.)

Figure 3.16 Leg lifts.

c   d

Figure 3.16 Leg lifts (cont.).

Plane Glide

Skate forward, gliding on your left skate with your right leg lifted behind you as high off the ice and as straight as possible. Extend the hockey stick horizontally in front of you. See how long you can maintain this position without putting the right skate down on the ice. It is harder to balance with the free leg behind you than in front of you. Beginners should do this gliding on the flat of the blade

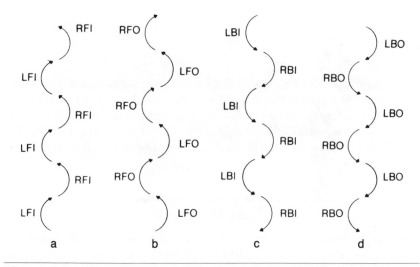

Figure 3.17   (a and b) Plane glide forward; (c and d) backward.

(Figure 3.16d). More advanced players should do it gliding on the inside, then outside edges. Figures 3.17a and b illustrate the exercise skating forward. Figures 3.17c and d illustrate the exercise skating backward.

Toe Touch

Glide on the flat of your left skate, holding the hockey stick in one hand. Stretch your right leg behind you, parallel to the ice. Keeping both your skating leg and free leg as straight as possible, reach down and try to touch the toe of your skating foot (Figure 3.18). Repeat, skating on the other foot. Be sure to keep the entire blade of your skating foot in contact with the ice surface. If you raise your heel off the ice, your weight will rock onto the curved toe and you may fall.

Figure 3.18   Toe touch.

This exercise demonstrates the importance of keeping the entire blade in contact with the ice. This is especially true when skating backward. Even though your weight is primarily on the front half of the blade when skating backward, do not allow the heel of the blade to lift off the ice, as this is a major cause of balance problems and falls.

Shoot the Duck

Squat over the right skate with your buttocks as close to the ice as possible. Your left leg should be off the ice, extended directly in front of you (Figure 3.19). Keep your back straight. If you lean too

Figure 3.19 Shoot the duck.

far forward from the waist, you won't be able to bend your knee to sit low enough. Experienced skaters should change feet while in this squatting position. Also, try to get up from this position without letting the free foot touch the ice. Try this exercise on each skate. This also is a good exercise for strengthening quadriceps (thigh) muscles, which increases your ability to flex your knees.

Jumps

This exercise is excellent for developing quadricep strength and knee bend, as well as for improving balance on the flats of the blades. Practice this exercise both forward and backward.

a   b

Figure 3.20 Jumps.

Glide on two skates. At the blue line start to jump from and land on both skates. Keep jumping until you reach the far blue line (Figures 3.20a and b).

Before each jump, bend your knees deeply so you are coiled to jump. Jump as high as possible. Cushion the landing by bending your knees deeply as you land. Keep your back straight as you land and avoid the tendency to bend forward from the waist, as this will pitch your weight over the curved toes of the blades. Keep your head up. Each time you land, be sure the entire blade lengths are in contact with the ice.

Hops

This exercise is excellent for developing quadricep strength and knee bend. It also helps develop balance and recovery abilities often called for in game situations.

Glide on one skate. At the blue line, start to hop on one skate. Keep hopping on the same skate until you reach the far blue line. Keep the other foot off the ice throughout the exercise.

Before each hop, deeply bend the knee of the hopping leg so you are coiled to jump. Jump as high as possible. Cushion the landing by deeply bending the knee of the landing leg (Figures 3.21a, b, and c). Keep your back straight as you land and avoid the tendency to bend forward from the waist, as this will pitch your weight over the curved toe of the blade. Keep your head up. Each time you land, be sure the entire blade length is in contact with the ice.

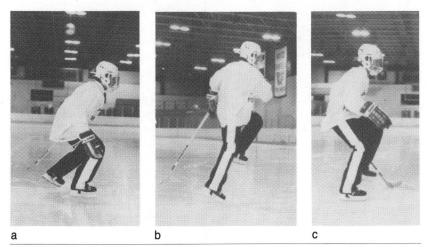

a   b   c

Figure 3.21 Hops.

Backward Cross Lifts—Alternating Feet

Hold your stick horizontally in front of you, chest high. Glide backward on the right inside edge and lift your left leg off the ice (Figures 3.22a and b). Raise your left leg up to touch the hockey stick while changing to the outside edge of your skating foot (Figure 3.22c). Next, bring your left foot down onto the ice, crossed in front of your right foot. Your left skate takes the ice on its inside edge (Figure 3.22d). Then repeat the procedure while skating on the left foot, lifting your right leg off the ice and raising it to touch the stick. Change to the LBO as you lift your right leg up to touch the stick, and then bring your right skate down onto the ice, crossed in front of your left foot on its inside edge. Keep repeating the exercise. Note that the line of travel changes as the edge changes. This drill can also be done skating forward.

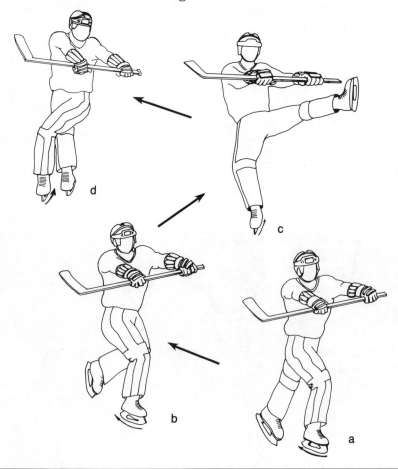

Figure 3.22   Backward cross lifts, alternating feet.

4

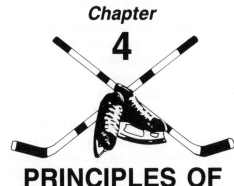

PRINCIPLES OF FORCE APPLICATION

Every sport requires precise and controlled application of force. Explosive force, well timed and properly executed, results in movement, either of an object (such as a puck, baseball, or football), an opponent, or you. Certain principles must be followed to produce optimum force. Although the end result in each sport may vary, the principles of force application are basically the same.

In skating, the explosive application of force (power) combines with rapid leg movement to produce speed. Speed is of vital concern to all hockey skaters.

Speed in skating can be defined as the distance each stride will carry you in a given time span. In hockey the time needed for a stride is approximated in fractions of a second. The distance covered depends largely on the correct and powerful application of force. Whether you are skating forward or backward or are executing crossover or starting maneuvers, the same principles apply. They must be learned, used, and timed correctly, and then combined with rapid leg movement.

Every stride consists of a push-glide sequence that involves a total transfer of body weight. Weight must be transferred from pushing edge to gliding edge and from gliding edge (or flat) to pushing edge with precision timing to achieve a smooth and efficient flowing motion.

Terms such as wind-up, follow-through, coil, recoil, spring, release, drive, thrust, and explode are commonly used throughout the sports world. These same terms effectively describe the basic components of hockey skating. The motions of every skating stride can be broken down into four distinct segments. Every stride, like the swing of a baseball bat, requires a *wind-up* or coiling action, a *release* or application of force from the coiled position, and a *follow-through* or completion of momentum. Skating requires an additional move as well: a *return* or recovery of the thrusting leg to a point under the body in preparation for the next stride. Try to separate every type of skating stride into these four segments: wind-up, release, follow-through, and return. If these principles are applied correctly, you will skate faster.

The Wind-Up

In skating, the wind-up corresponds to the backswing of the baseball bat. It acts to "coil the spring." The more coiling action, the more force available upon release. This coiling action is achieved by digging in the edge of the thrusting skate at a strong angle to the ice (approximately 45 degrees), bending both knees (90 degrees), and pressing the body weight down over the gripping edge. This allows the edge to grip the ice strongly. Without the thrusting edge gripping and the body weight pressing down over it, there will be no traction. The skate will slip and slide rather than cut into the ice.

Figure 4.1 The wind-up.

The more edge used to dig into the ice and the more the body weight presses downward over the edge, the more grip available to release (push) against. Figure 4.1 shows an effective wind-up with edge, knee, and body weight pressing strongly into the ice in preparation for a push on the forward stride.

The Release

The release is the actual leg thrust that drives against the ice and causes movement. It can be compared to the actual swinging of the baseball bat. The more efficiently and rapidly the legs thrust, the more power and speed achieved. Many hockey players are unaware of just how hard their legs must push (uncoil) to get maximum speed. It is hard work!

In a good release the pushing leg, with the body weight centered over it, pushes quickly, forcefully, and directly against the cutting edge, which is wedged into the ice (Figures 4.2a and b).

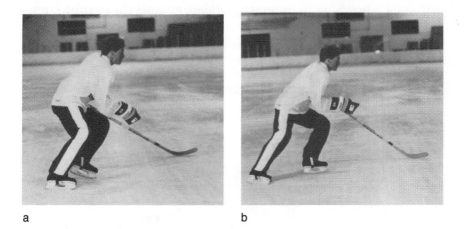

a   b

Figure 4.2   The release.

There is a general rule for thrusting that holds true for almost every maneuver in skating: Each push must be executed so that the thrusting leg pushes directly against the *entire length* of the blade, which is digging into the ice at an acute angle of approximately 45 degrees (Figures 4.3a and b). This is true regardless of the direction the thrusting blade is facing, which varies according to the maneuver being performed. The leg must exert its force in

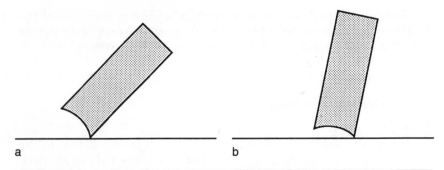

Figure 4.3   (a) A 45-degree angle of edge to ice sets up an effective thrust and allows the body weight to project low and forward; (b) a greater angle results in a weak push and causes upward body motion.

a line perpendicular to that described by the blade's length—perpendicular to the grip, in other words. Figures 4.4a-e show the way the blade should face during various maneuvers and the resultant directions of leg drive.

Remember that when thrusting you are actually pushing yourself, your entire weight, not just your leg, against the cutting edge.

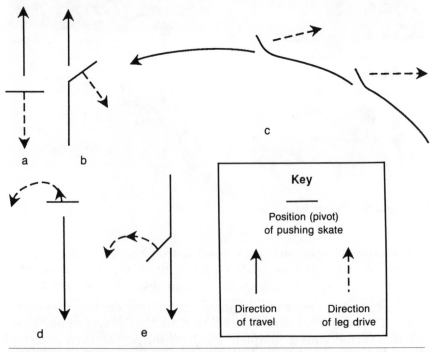

Figure 4.4   Pushing against the edge: (a) forward (front) start; (b) forward stride; (c) crossovers; (d) backward start; (e) backward stride.

To accomplish this, you must have your weight centered over the thrusting leg. Only at the midpoint of the push does the body weight shift from the pushing foot onto the other (gliding) foot.

The Follow-Through

Thrusting the legs without following through is like swinging the baseball bat and then halting as the bat meets the ball. In skating, incomplete leg drive results in a loss of power, and therefore of speed. Every push in skating requires a follow-through with the thrusting leg fully extended away from the body with the hip, knee, and toe locked. The gliding leg must maintain a deep knee bend as the thrusting leg extends. Only when fully extended has the pushing leg followed through to completion. The toe of the thrusting blade just barely clears the ice (see Figures 4.5a and b). In backward skating, the skate actually stays on the ice. Many players move their legs too fast and do not allow them to reach full extension.

a   b

Figure 4.5   The follow-through.

As a result, they never reach top speed. Moving the legs fast without full leg drive is counterproductive. Hockey players must first learn to thrust with a complete leg drive for power, then practice this taking their strides quickly. This combination of power plus rapid leg motion results in optimal speed.

The Return (Recovery)

The return is a critical and often neglected aspect of the stride. After reaching full extension, the thrusting leg must return, by reversing its outward path, to center under the body. This ensures that the entire body weight can be placed over the foot now preparing to push. The return must be rapid with the skate staying close to the ice as the leg returns. In backward striding the skate actually stays on the ice as the leg returns. A straight-line path of return is most effective in forward striding; a circular path takes longer, delaying the next stride. However, a circular path is necessary in backward striding because of the technique involved in the push/return portions of the stride. A rapid return also requires that the knee of the gliding leg stays well bent during the return, to prevent the body from popping or bouncing up between strides. Such pop-ups cause a delay between strides. A slow leg recovery, or a recovery where the leg is high off the ice on the return, will negatively affect the ability to move the legs rapidly. Figures 4.6a and b show the proper return of the leg during the forward stride.

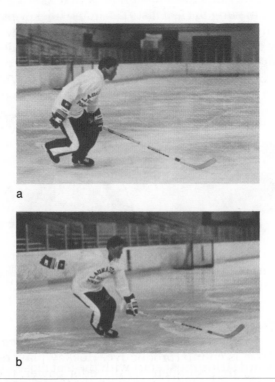

a

b

Figure 4.6   The return.

5

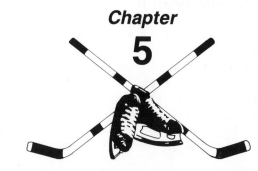

THE FORWARD STRIDE

A common and serious misconception is that skating fast is synonymous with moving the feet fast. Too many hockey players move their feet with trip-hammer speed but neglect to apply force effectively. As a result, they move as if on a treadmill, perpetually working, but going nowhere fast.

Speed is a combination of power and quickness, so while it is true that you need rapid leg motion to build up speed, you must also learn how to use the blade edges, your legs, and your body weight correctly and powerfully. You must also learn to take advantage of the glide of the skate once you have accelerated. This will be discussed later in this chapter (see "Glide of the Forward Stride").

All strides are technically alike. The basic difference between them is merely the length of the glide—how long you spend gliding before the next foot takes the ice. There should be no difference in the amount of force exerted on each thrust or in the techniques of leg drive, weight shift, and leg recovery.

Following is a description of each segment of the forward stride. The second part of the chapter includes exercises for each segment.

The Wind-Up

1. Each forward stride must start with the feet close together and well centered under your body, with the thrusting foot pivoted

outward so that your feet form a V. Figure 5.1a shows a wide V used when starting or skating slowly. Figure 5.1b shows a narrow V used when skating with greater speed.

2. Press the inside edge of the thrusting (right) foot into the ice so the skate blade and lower leg form approximately a 45-degree angle with the ice.

3. Bend both knees deeply and press your body weight over and slightly to the inside of your thrusting foot (Figure 5.2a). At this instant your hips should be positioned over the pushing foot and your chest above the toe of the pushing foot.

a   b

Figure 5.1   The V position.

The Release

1. The release of the thrusting leg, directly out against the inside edge of the blade, will be to the back and side. The precise direction is determined by the position of the edge on the ice. Thrust directly against the grip, using the entire blade length to push. Start the push with the heel of the inside edge and finish with the toe of the inside edge (Figures 5.2b and c). This heel-to-toe push requires you to use the entire length of the rockered blade: Shift your weight from the back to the front of the inside blade edge during the push.

2. As you thrust with your right leg, your left foot will take the ice and receive the weight you are shifting from the pushing foot, and will become the gliding foot. This transfer of weight onto the gliding foot takes place approximately midway through the push (Figure 5.2b). If you shift your weight too soon, or if weight is not shifted forward and outward properly, momentum and power will be lost.

3. Although your leg performs the actual thrust, the purpose in pushing is to drive your total body weight against the blade edge gripping the ice.

4. The main power of the thrust is provided by the thigh muscles. If your thigh muscles don't feel the strain of each push they are not being fully employed. Terms for pushing hard include "explode off your pushing leg," "deliver a knockout punch," "go full throttle," and "gun the motor."

   Most hockey players get accustomed to pushing with a certain amount of force, believing it to be their maximum effort. Usually, however, they are capable of pushing much harder. Experimentation is essential to developing a more powerful and effective thrust.

5. Do not push straight backward, as in running, as this will cause you to push mainly from the front tip of the blade, which gives little traction and causes a slip of the skate rather than a thrust. You cannot get power from a slip. Pushing sideways as well as back will give you a better grip and more power.

6. The gliding skate must point slightly outward as it takes the ice, and the body weight, when shifting onto the gliding skate, must shift out over it. During the glide the skate and body weight must then be rolled onto and above the inside edge in preparation for pushing. These changes result in an outward followed by an inward shift of weight on each stride. (See "The Glide of the Forward Stride," later in this chapter.)

The Follow-Through

1. Continue thrusting your leg against the inside edge until it reaches full extension. At the end of the thrust the hip and knee should snap into a locked position. This instant coincides with the final thrust (from the toe of the inside edge) against the ice (Figure 5.2d). This final thrust from the front of the inside edge is sometimes referred to by hockey players as the "toe flick." The snap of the ankle and inside edge of the toe against the ice gives the thrust a powerful finish.

Figure 5.2 Forward stride sequence.

(cont.)

i   j

Figure 5.2   Forward stride sequence (cont.).

2. As the thrusting leg reaches full extension and leaves the ice, it becomes the free leg. Keep the free foot and knee in a turned out position, the toe reaching down to within about 1 inch of the ice (Figure 5.2d). Raising your free foot higher than that raises your center of gravity, breaking your forward momentum and delaying the recovery. "Toeing down," or pushing off with the tip instead of the edge of the blade (caused by loss of turnout of the knee and toe), results in the heel kicking up in a running motion, with a resultant loss of power.

3. As the free leg completes its extension, the knee of your gliding leg should stay well bent (about 90 degrees). A properly bent gliding knee will be out ahead of that same toe. If the leg is straight or only moderately bent, your center of gravity will be too high. This hinders both stability and speed (Figure 5.3). The amount of knee bend of the gliding leg also determines how far you can thrust your pushing leg against the ice and away

Figure 5.3   Incorrect: gliding knee not bent sufficiently.

from your body. A deep knee bend allows you to push farther, producing more speed.
4. At full extension there is a straight line of force from the shoulders through the thrusting hip, leg, knee, ankle, and toe. At this instant the proper body position for the forward stride is gliding knee ahead of gliding toe, chest over gliding knee, hips square and level to ice (facing line of travel), back straight, head up, arms moving in line and in unison with the legs. At top speed the angle of the body (trunk) to the ice is approximately 45 degrees (Figure 5.4).

Figure 5.4 Straight line of force and alignment of body at full extension.

The Return

The return of the leg coincides with the shift of the body weight toward the inside of the gliding foot.

1. For the return, pull your free (right) leg back to its original position under your body. The leg should reverse its outward path. Keep the skate close to the ice, with the knee and toe still turned out as the leg returns (Figure 5.2e). A straight-line recovery is most effective.
2. As the free leg returns, maintain a deep knee bend on the gliding leg. Straightening the knee even a little impairs your momentum. It also slows the recovery of the free leg and delays the next push.
3. As the free skate returns, it should momentarily meet your gliding foot (left) in a V position and then immediately pass by it (about three quarters of a blade length) to take the ice as the gliding skate (Figure 5.2f).

Execute the next push as follows:

1. As your free foot draws under your body in the V position, your gliding foot will already be pivoted outward and prepared to push. Dig its inside edge into the ice at an approximate 45-degree angle, using a deep knee bend.
2. Place your weight over the inside edge of the left skate, and repeat with that leg the above procedure of wind-up, release, follow-through, and return (Figures 5.2g, h, i, and j). You have completed one cycle when you are again gliding on the original foot.

The Glide of the Forward Stride

Often debated is whether the glide of the forward hockey stride begins on the flat of the blade or on the outside edge of the blade. From the curved pattern of the glide it appears to be on an outside edge. But the curve could be a result of the outward direction of the gliding skate as it takes the ice and the subsequent transfer of body weight over the blade.

If the glide does begin on the outside edge it is minimal and of short duration. The edge must change almost immediately. The majority of the glide is on the flat of the blade. Then, in preparation for pushing, the skate and body weight must be rolled onto and above the inside edge.

Regardless of whether this actually occurs, it is a useful way of thinking of the glide. This is because an outside edge can be achieved only when the skating foot takes the ice under the body. Gliding momentarily on the outside edge will encourage you to return your free leg properly, with the free foot (the foot preparing to become the gliding foot) centered under your body. This makes for a more efficient thrust from the pushing leg and better weight transfer from pushing leg to gliding leg, and greater flow in the desired direction (Figure 5.5a). Figure 5.5b shows strides that are the result of lateral motion caused by incomplete return of the free leg prior to pushing.

The Arm Swing

Many skaters believe that by swinging their arms vigorously they will skate faster. When the arms are used correctly that is so.

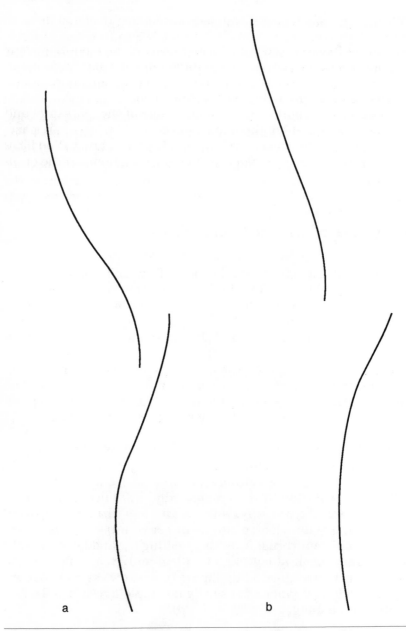

Figure 5.5 The glide of the forward stride: (a) correct; (b) incorrect—incomplete leg recovery.

But speed in skating comes primarily from your legs. Your arms provide rhythm and forward drive but they are not the prime source of speed. They should be used in addition to the legs, not as a substitution.

Move your arms forward and backward along diagonal lines, in rhythm with your legs. Arms must match legs in terms of force, direction of movement, and range of motion. As in running, the right arm drives forward as the right leg drives back. Your upper body should not twist from side to side, and your shoulders should stay level with the ice and not move excessively. Your elbows should pass close to your ribs and finish with one extending diagonally forward and the other extending diagonally back. An imaginary line is formed between the right arm and foot and between the left hand and foot (Figure 5.6). The arm swing should not cross the midline of your body. Swinging your arms from side to side or across the midline of your body encourages lateral motion and creates upper body twist (Figure 5.7).

Figure 5.6   Correct arm swing: forward/backward motion.

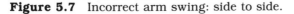

Figure 5.7   Incorrect arm swing: side to side.

One myth among hockey players is that you should always skate with both hands on the stick. Not true. There are certain instances when it is important to keep only the top hand on the stick—for example, when you do not have the puck and are skating straight ahead or are trying to break out with the puck. At such times holding the stick with both hands and keeping the stick on the ice slows you unnecessarily. Likewise, skating with both hands on the stick and the stick in the air often leads to the habit of swinging the arms from side to side. This impedes speed and makes it difficult to take passes, because the stick blade is off the ice.

Practice skating forward with only your top hand holding the stick, and the stick blade on the ice. Extend your arms through their swing as you skate. Locking and keeping the elbows close to the body will restrict your ability to move. Since the arms and legs work cooperatively, extending the arms helps you extend the legs.

POINTS TO REMEMBER

- Begin and end each push with feet in an approximate V position.
- Keep weight low and angled forward for optimum motion.
- To maintain speed and momentum, keep your gliding knee well bent throughout the stride.
- Thrust pushing leg to the back and side, directly against the entire length of the inside edge.
- Start each push with your pushing leg centered under your body. Finish each push with that leg fully extended away from your body. Prepare for the next push by returning that leg to center under the body. These combined movements constitute full range of motion of the pushing leg.
- Once you begin to move the legs through their full range of motion, practice doing this at progressively faster tempos.
- Keep your hips facing straight ahead and level to the ice.
- Keep your head up. Look ahead, not down! Don't move it from side to side.
- Keep shoulders, back, chest up, back straight. If you hunch over you will be off balance.

- Goalies must master all skating moves, especially the forward stride. The techniques for pushing across the goal crease are the same (Figures 5.8a, b, and c).

a

b

c

Figure 5.8   Goalie utilizing forward stride across goal crease.

Exercises for Improving the Forward Stride

These exercises for improving the forward stride are subdivided into exercises for each segment of the stride.

Wind-Up Exercises

The purpose of these exercises is to learn and practice the mechanics of executing an effective wind-up.

The Coil

This exercise is done standing in place. Perform this exercise first standing on the right foot, then on the left.

1. Place your feet in the V position, heels together, toes apart.
2. Dig in the inside edge of your right skate and bend your right knee so that your ankle and lower leg form a 45-degree angle to the ice. The boot will lean halfway down to the ice.
3. Put all your weight on your right foot.
4. Lift your left foot, balancing in place on your right inside edge. Do not allow the edge angle to change (Figure 5.9).

This exercise should make you feel both the amount of pressure needed to dig the edge into the ice at the angle needed to push effectively, as well as the strain of maintaining that edge while the other foot is off the ice. Remember: Foot, ankle, knee, and body weight must all work together to provide a strong cutting edge.

Figure 5.9   The coil exercise: standing on an inside edge.

Flat-to-Inside Edge

This exercise is done skating at a moderate pace: Speed is not the issue here. The idea is to develop the edging capability demanded for an effective thrust. It is done first with one foot, then with the other. Do not put both feet on the ice at the same time.

1. Glide forward on your left foot, on the flat of the blade, right foot off the ice.

2. Keeping all your weight on your left foot, and your right foot off the ice, quickly roll your left ankle inward and bend your left knee so that the inside edge cuts into the ice at a 45-degree angle.

3. The sudden dropping of the inside edge into the ice will form a semicircular cut (Figure 5.10a) in the ice and you will curve sharply clockwise. Now push off from your left leg and skate onto your right foot. Repeat the exercise (Figure 5.10b). This time the sudden dropping of the inside edge will curve you sharply counterclockwise. Keep repeating, skating from one foot to the other, for the length of the ice. Figure 5.11 shows a player curving sharply on the inside edge of the right skate.

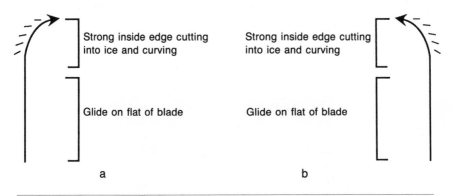

Figure 5.10   Flat-to-inside-edge exercise: (a) left foot; (b) right foot.

Figure 5.11   Player curving sharply on inside edge.

The action of going from the flat to a strong inside edge simulates that instant in the stride when the gliding foot rolls inward onto a strong inside edge in preparation for becoming the new thrusting foot. If the skate blade does not roll in to a sufficient angle to the ice, the skate will not cut into the ice to form the sharp curve. If this happens you will skid as in a stop.

Release Exercises

The purpose of these exercises is to teach the mechanics of executing an effective wind-up and release, as well as to improve the use of inside edges, knees, leg drive, and body weight, and to push more effectively.

Resistance Exercise

1. Face another player, holding a stick horizontally between you.
2. You, as the player going forward, must push the other player backward. The other skater should try to prevent you from moving by doing a two-foot backward snowplow stop (see chapter 9).
3. To move the resisting skater, turn your feet into an exaggerated V position with heels together and toes apart. Then dig in hard with the inside edges, bend your knees and press your weight down as hard as possible.

Each leg should drive to full extension and then return to the V position in preparation for the next thrust. Without good edging

Figure 5.12   Resistance exercise.

and leg drive you will not move the resisting player. Keep shoulders back and head up as you push your partner across the ice (Figure 5.12). The idea is for you, the forward skater, to have to work your legs exceptionally hard to move the backward skater. This will force you to dig into the ice more and to push harder than you have had to do before.

Don't try to go fast. The object is to feel the actual working of the edges, knees, and body weight; to develop powerful leg drive; and to become accustomed to feeling the cutting action of the blades before each thrust. When skating normally you should use the same amount of edge, downward pressure, and leg drive as you do when pushing a resisting skater.

NOTE: This drill is also used as a wind-up and follow-through drill.

One Leg Push

Start at the sideboards, skating forward across the ice. Use only your right leg as the thrusting leg each time you push. To prepare for each push, dig the inside edge of the blade into the ice at a 45-degree angle, bend the pushing knee deeply, and press your body weight down over the edge as in the previous exercise. Thrust your pushing leg as hard as you can to full extension on every push and return the leg completely before pushing again.

Coming back across the ice, use only your left leg to thrust. Many skaters are stronger and more coordinated on one side of the body than the other, so one leg often thrusts more effectively. The idea is for both legs to eventually become equal in strength through constant repetition of this and other exercises. Always emphasize the weak side.

Variation: Do the same exercise, using only four pushes to reach the opposite boards. Recover the pushing leg rapidly after each thrust to avoid excessive gliding. The goal is to build up speed on each of the four pushes so that after each push you are traveling faster than you were on the previous push.

Drag/Touch

Do the One Leg Push, but on each stride drag the inside edge of the toe on the ice at the finish of the push. Also, keep the toe (inside edge) of the blade on the ice as you return the leg under your body. On the return, the heel of the returning foot should touch the heel of the gliding foot. Keep the knee of the gliding leg well bent as you return the free leg, and maintain the turnout of the knee and toe of the free leg as it returns.

Follow-Through Exercises

Use these exercises to learn the mechanics of executing an effective follow-through.

Resistance Exercise

The Resistance Exercise described under "Release Exercises" can also be used as a follow-through exercise. Perform it in the same way.

Snap/Stretch

The purpose of this exercise is to develop an understanding of what you should feel when the pushing leg is fully extended. It is done standing in place.

1. Stand in the V position: heels together, toes apart.
2. Bend both knees deeply, keeping your back straight (Figure 5.13a).
3. Quickly straighten both legs so that both knees lock. Hold your legs locked and feel the tightness in your leg muscles; there

a   b   c

Figure 5.13 Snap/stretch exercise.

is no crease behind your knees (Figure 5.13b). This is how the pushing leg should feel when fully extended.

4. Do the same thing, only this time keep the knee of one leg well bent and snap the other leg out to the back and side (grazing the ice rather than digging into it) until it is locked. The snapped leg is the pushing leg. When locked, it is in the position of the fully extended leg during the forward skating stride (Figure 5.13c). Keep the leg locked and sense the tightness of the muscles in the leg and the amount of stretch between your legs. Be sure the knee and toe are in the turned out position. Repeat with the other leg.

Bend/Extend

The purpose of this exercise is to practice keeping the knee of the gliding leg bent while the free leg is fully extended.

1. Starting at the goal line, skate forward to the first blue line.
2. At the blue line, thrust your right leg out against the inside edge, and glide on your left leg. Maintain a deep knee bend of the left knee (about 90 degrees); the knee should be out ahead of the toe. Thrust your right leg to full extension and hold it there with the right knee locked, knee and toe turned out, and the toe held about 1 inch off the ice (Figure 5.14).

Figure 5.14 Bend/extend exercise.

3. Hold this position and glide on your left leg to the far blue line. When you reach the far blue line resume skating to the far end of the ice.
4. Keep your back straight. Incline your body, so that your chest lines up above your front knee. Hold the hockey stick with just the top hand.
5. Repeat the drill coming back down the ice, now using the left leg as the thrusting leg and the right leg as the gliding leg.

Toe Drag

This drill emphasizes what you should feel when the leg is fully extended and accents the correct use of the toe to finish the push (toe flick).

Skate forward down the ice. At the completion of each thrust, drag the inside edge of the toe of your pushing leg on the ice. The leg should be locked and fully extended, with the knee and toe turned out, as you drag in the toe (Figure 5.15). Return the pushing leg, keeping the toe turned out, dragging it on the ice as the leg returns. Return the leg until the heel touches the heel of the gliding foot, then push with the other leg and do the same thing. Move your legs rapidly to avoid excessive gliding.

Figure 5.15   Toe drag exercise.

On every forward stride you should experience for an instant a tightening of the muscles of the hip, thigh, knee, ankle, and toe of your pushing leg when it is locked and fully extended. This tightening indicates that you have reached complete extension, and that your toe is reaching down toward the ice after the final toe flick.

Be sure the toe is turned outward, not pointed straight down at the ice. Also be sure to keep the knee of the gliding leg well bent and out ahead of the gliding toe as you return the free leg.

The C-Cut

This exercise is called the C-cut because in it the skate describes a C-shaped arc or loop on the ice alongside the skater. The leg moves first to the rear, curves out to extend sideways, passes forward, and completes the arc by curving back to its starting position beneath the midline of the body. The exercise incorporates numerous important skating and training fundamentals:

- Using the inside edges to cut forcefully into the ice when pushing.
- Thrusting to the back and side rather than directly back.
- Compelling your body to experience a fully extended, straight free leg resulting from a maximum-effort thrust, rather than a less extended, weaker push.
- Training the gliding and pushing legs to work independently of each other, so that you glide straight ahead on a well bent knee while pushing to the back and side and then locking the thrusting leg.
- Using the entire blade length for thrust. (Start each push with the heel, finish with the toe.) In all skating maneuvers, controlling the rock of the blade is as important as controlling the edges. As you learn to distribute your weight on specific points along the rock of the blade, you will develop greater agility and maneuverability.
- Determining the difference in effectiveness and coordination between your strong leg and weak leg so that you can equalize them.
- Conditioning the quadriceps. The C-cut exercise requires proper use of thigh muscles.
- Understanding how to execute backward thrusts effectively. The leg motion in backward skating is exactly the reverse of the forward C-cut push (see chapter 7).
- Preparing for more difficult maneuvers such as the pivot (see chapter 8), which is based on the ability to do a C-cut.

The forward C-cut, diagrammed in Figure 5.16, is skated with both feet on the ice at all times. The exercise begins with the left leg as the pushing leg.

1. Glide on the flats of both skates, feet directly under your body. Keep your back straight.

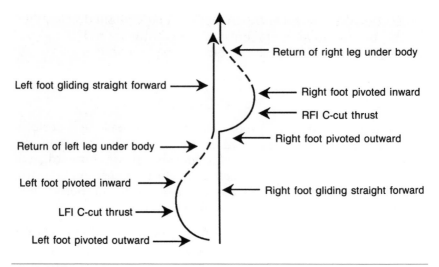

Return of right leg under body

Left foot gliding straight forward

Right foot pivoted inward

RFI C-cut thrust

Right foot pivoted outward

Return of left leg under body

Left foot pivoted inward

Right foot gliding straight forward

LFI C-cut thrust

Left foot pivoted outward

Figure 5.16   Pattern of the forward C-cut.

2. Prepare to push with your left leg, gliding straight ahead on the flat of your right skate.

3. Keep your weight on the back half of the thrusting skate.

4. Bend your knees and dig the inside edge of your left skate into the ice, so that the skate and lower leg form a 45-degree angle to the ice, and press your body weight down over the edge. At the same time, pivot your left foot so that your feet approximate a right angle: heels together, toes apart. You are now prepared to push.

5. Cut the letter C into the ice with your left skate, starting at the bottom end of the C. Push first to the back, then out to the side, then forward, then finally around to its starting point under your body. Thrust hard. (See Figures 5.17a through e.)

6. At the midpoint of the C-cut thrust, transfer your weight onto the flat of your gliding (right) skate.

7. Thrust powerfully and to full extension. Keep the thrusting skate on the ice after the thrust is completed. Note that the knee of the gliding leg remains well bent even when the thrusting leg is fully extended.

8. After full extension, your left foot must glide back to a position underneath your body to prepare for the next push. To accomplish this, pigeon-toe your left foot and draw it toward your right foot. After the return, your feet will be side by side and centered under your body (Figure 5.17f).

9. The left leg should be straight and fully extended to the side when you are in the middle of the C, but it must be coiled well

a   b   c

d   e   f

Figure 5.17   Forward C-cut sequence.

under your body at the beginning and end points, which correspond respectively to the coil and return of each thrust. Keep the knee of the gliding leg well bent as you return the pushing leg.

10. After its return, your left foot becomes the gliding foot. Put your weight on the inside edge of your right skate and cut a reverse letter C on that side, starting from the bottom end of the C: Push to the back, then out to the side, forward, around, and then in under your body.

POINTS TO REMEMBER

- Keep your hips square (facing straight ahead). If your hips turn sideways or wiggle, you will skate from side to side rather than straight ahead. This will prevent you from achieving a full stride and will affect your forward motion.
- The gliding foot must aim straight ahead and glide on the flat of the blade while the thrusting foot pivots and cuts the C and returns. If both feet turn the same way you will skate an S formation rather than a straight line.

Variation:

Do the drill holding your stick horizontally in the crooks of your elbows, behind your back (Figure 5.18). Do not let the stick move around. This variation eliminates use of the arms and shoulders and forces the legs to do all the work.

Figure 5.18 Forward C-cut, arms behind back.

Return Exercises

Use these exercises to learn the mechanics of an effective return.

Snap/Click

This exercise is done standing in place.

1. Keeping the knee of your standing leg well bent, snap the pushing leg out to the back and side until it is locked.
2. Return the "pushing" leg back under your body, until that heel clicks against the heel of your standing foot. As your heels click, your feet should take the V position. Remember to maintain the turnout of the knee and toe through the return. Return the leg so that it reverses its outward path (Figure 5.19).
3. Keep the knee of your standing leg well bent as your pushing leg returns and as your heels click together.
4. Repeat, using the other leg as the pushing leg.
5. Keep repeating the exercise to develop the correct return motion.

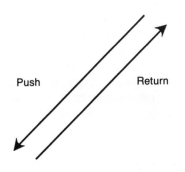

Push   Return

Figure 5.19   Push/return.

NOTE: Although when you are striding the heels should not actually touch, they should be very close together.

Push/Click

Skate forward. At each stride concentrate on returning the pushing leg so that your heels click together, feet in the V formation. Be sure to drive the leg directly against the inside edge and return it along a straight path that retraces the outward path (see Figure 5.19).

By making the heels actually touch you will develop the feeling of how far in to bring the free leg so that it is centered under your body for the next push.

The Rapid Stride Versus the Long Stride

All strides should be long strides—in other words, they should all be *full* strides. The rapid stride is called such because of the fast leg rhythm used. The difference between it and a long stride is the length of the glide rather than technique, leg extension, or effort expended in pushing. The thrusting leg must still drive to full extension and return fully under the body even when leg motion is very rapid. The rapidity of the stride is determined simply by how quickly the legs move as they push and recover. Rapid strides are comparable to sprint running, when a sudden burst of speed over a relatively short distance is required.

Playing hockey often requires rapid strides. For instance, rapid strides are necessary for acceleration (such as when you are skating slowly and need to speed up suddenly, when you burst out on a breakaway, or for an explosive start). There are, however, occasions when you will want to use a longer, slower stride (a longer glide): for example, when you have reached top speed and want to maintain it while conserving energy, or when you do not need to skate at top speed. In these situations your strides are technically the same, but your legs move slower. In other words, all strides should be full strides!

Exercises for Stride Tempos

Since all strides are really long strides (full strides), we will refer to "long glides" rather than long strides. The main purpose of these exercises is to produce correct technique at varying stride tempos, and to develop balance and control at all stride tempos.

Long Glides

This exercise is done as you skate around the entire rink. Skate in a counterclockwise direction. Pick up speed on the corners by using crossovers, and as you approach the blue line, use rapid strides.

At the first blue line, however, thrust just once with your right leg and then glide on your left foot until you reach the red line. Keep your free leg fully extended until you reach the red line. At the red line, repeat, switching legs: thrust with your left leg and glide on your right foot, keeping your free leg fully extended until you reach the next blue line. The idea is to maintain speed and balance for the entire glide. If you use the edges properly and thrust hard, you should be able to maintain speed on the glide.

When you reach the second blue line, use rapid strides to skate to the far end of the ice and then crossovers to skate the corners and build up speed again. When you are back at the first blue line on the other side of the ice, repeat the long glides. Move your arms diagonally forward and back in line with and in rhythm with your legs, and keep your hockey stick on the ice, holding it with just your top hand.

Also do the exercise skating around the rink in a clockwise direction.

NOTE: Small skaters should use two strides from blue line to red line, and two strides from red line to blue line.

Varying Stride Tempos

Start at the goal line and skate down the ice, varying stride tempos as follows: Between the goal line and the near blue line, take eight to ten rapid strides. From blue line to blue line, take four strides. Between far blue line and far goal line, take only two. Maintain speed even when doing the very long glides, and be sure you always push to full extension. Move your arms diagonally forward and backward in line with and in rhythm with your legs, and keep your hockey stick on the ice, holding it with just your top hand.

NOTE: The number of strides needed may vary. For example, younger players may need twelve, six and three strides respectively from goal line to blue line, blue line to blue line and blue line to goal line; advanced players may need fewer than the numbers given.

Stride and Control

This excellent exercise for stride and control is similar to the exercise for long glides (skate counterclockwise), except that immediately after you come out of the corner and reach the face-off circle take one very hard thrust (using your right leg to thrust and your left leg to glide) and glide all the way to the center red line. At the red line thrust with your left leg, and glide on your right until you reach the face-off circle at the far end of the ice. Skate hard around the corner (crossovers) to build up speed, then repeat. Keep your free leg fully extended during the glides. Again, use powerful, rapid crossovers to build up your speed on the corners. This exercise also helps improve balance on glides.

NOTE: This exercise uses only two strides for the length of the ice from face-off circle to face-off circle. Try to maintain speed on the two long glides. This exercise demands extremely powerful thrusts, excellent balance and control, and powerful, rapid crossovers on the corners. Younger skaters may need to take four or six strides for each length of the ice. Again, the numbers are an approximation and depend upon age and ability.

Rapid Leg Speed

After learning to thrust properly and powerfully, you may find that your legs push effectively but do not move quickly enough. It is imperative that you develop leg speed along with correct technique and power. The combination of correct, powerful thrust and rapid leg motion is the key to speed.

NOTE: In addition to quickness training (see chapter 12), skating to music is an effective way to build leg speed. Use music with a fast tempo. Try to move your legs in time to the music, but remember to get maximum power and full range of motion on each stride.

Varying Leg Speeds

To improve your versatility, practice skating powerfully to many different tempos of music. This will also help you skate rhythmically. Swing your arms in a diagonal forward/backward motion, in line and in rhythm with your legs.

Leg rhythm is slightly different for each person. The rhythm varies according to one's body type and leg length. Small and tall players will have different styles and leg rhythms. Some tall players move their legs overly fast for their leg length, and thus reduce their ability to achieve full range of motion. Concentrate on developing full range of motion and a powerful leg drive with rapid recovery of the free leg. Move your legs as rapidly as possible while doing this. But your leg rhythm should be adjusted to your body type and leg length.

Restricting the Arms

Restricting the use of your arms during stride exercises can help emphasize and develop correct use of the legs, especially when stickhandling. Too many players slow down when they skate with the puck because they have not trained their legs to work without the aid of their arms. The following exercises can be used to restrict arm movement and train the legs to work independently of the arms.

Exercise 1

Skate forward, holding your hockey stick horizontally behind your back in the crooks of your elbows to prevent your arms from moving. Or, use no stick at all and clasp your hands on your stomach or behind your back. You can also hold the stick horizontally with your arms extended straight out in front of you, chest high. Keep your upper body still and your chest facing straight ahead while skating in these positions.

Exercise 2

Practice skating at top speed with both hands on the stick and the stick on the ice out in front of you (Figure 5.20) and then while controlling the puck. Push powerfully and rapidly and try to achieve speed from your legs alone.

Figure 5.20 Restricting the arms by holding hockey stick with both hands.

Chapter

6

THE BACKWARD STRIDE

The ability to skate straight backward with speed and mobility is critical not only for defenders who must cover their team's flanks against the oncoming foe, but for all members of the team. All players from time to time must play defense, and they must do so effectively or give the other team a distinct advantage.

Some players like to skate backward using only backward crossovers, feeling they can go faster that way than when skating straight backward. However, backward crossovers can be dangerous in game situations, for a defender who crosses over prematurely becomes commited to moving in that direction. A forward will look for that error, cut the other way, and get by the defender.

Backward crossovers are commonly used to accelerate. Once you build up speed, however, you should skate straight backward so you can stay directly in front of the oncoming forward with your feet in a neutral position. You will then be able to stay with the forward and move to either side to block or check him or her.

As in the straight forward stride, rapid leg movement alone does not ensure speed. It must be combined with the power and drive achieved from using edges, legs, and body weight correctly. When skating straight backward, the leg performs the C-cut push, done in reverse of the forward C-cut push described in chapter 5. The push is now from the top of the C to the front, then outward, down, and back around to the end point of the C.

The four-part procedure of wind-up, release, follow-through, and return is as important to power and speed here as it is in the forward stride. Keep in mind that the proper use of edges, knee bend, body weight, weight shift, and glide that is necessary for speed when skating forward is also necessary for speed when skating backward.

The Wind-Up

As in all skating moves, each push begins with a coiling action. To initiate the push of the backward stride, the thrusting foot must be centered under your body weight and must dig into the ice on a strong inside edge. Your knees must be well bent and your shoulders held back. When skating backward your back should be held in a fairly vertical position and your weight should be on the front halves of the blades.

1. Put your weight on your pushing (left) foot and bend your knees deeply—the knee of your pushing foot should be out ahead of that toe.
2. Pivot your pushing (left) foot, heel outward, to a position so that your feet approximate a right angle (toes together, heels apart). Pivoting the pushing foot is critical to the C-cut thrust.
3. Dig the inside edge of your left skate into the ice by rolling in your ankle and bending your knee so that the skate and lower leg form an approximate 45-degree angle to the ice (Figure 6.1). This completes the wind-up.

Figure 6.1   The pivot of the backward C-cut.

The Release

1. Using the inside edge of your left skate, cut the letter C into the ice. Use the front half of the blade to push. The push starts from the top of the C and cuts first to the front and then out to the side. Drive your leg powerfully out against the edge, using a forceful snapping action of the leg (Figure 6.2a).
2. At approximately the midpoint of the C-cut thrust, transfer your body weight onto your gliding (right) foot. Because you are skating backward, your body weight should be situated over the front half of your gliding foot, though the entire blade length must be in contact with the ice.
3. Thrust to full extension of the pushing leg.

a   b   c

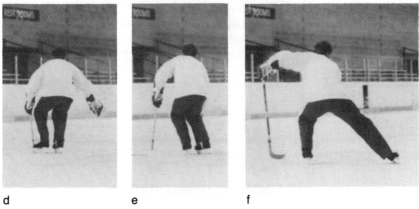

d   e   f

Figure 6.2   Backward stride sequence.

The Follow-Through

1. Thrust until the leg is fully extended. The final thrust comes from the front (toe) of the inside edge. The locking of the pushing leg coincides with the toe flick of the inside edge. This combination constitutes an effective follow-through (Figure 6.2b). Much experimenting is necessary to find your point of full extension.
2. Keep the thrusting (left) foot on the ice after the thrust is completed.
3. Keep your gliding knee well bent even when the thrusting leg is fully extended.
4. Be sure the gliding skate continues to point straight backward; glide on the flat of the blade as the thrusting leg pushes.

The Return

1. After your leg reaches full extension, the pushing (left) foot must return quickly to a position directly under your body to prepare for the next push. To return the leg, pivot the left heel inward. Then draw the left foot under your hips to complete the C (Figures 6.2c and d), keeping the skate on the ice as it returns.
2. When the leg has completed its return, your feet should be side by side and almost parallel to each other. Do not allow the pushing leg to get behind your gliding foot. This will pull your hips to the side, forcing you to skate a snakelike pattern.
3. Once your left foot has returned it is prepared to become the new gliding foot, while your right foot is prepared to thrust the C-cut push. On the right leg thrust the C will be formed in reverse. Put your weight over your right foot, bend your knees, and pivot your right heel outward (Figure 6.2e). Then mirror the above procedure to execute the right C-cut thrust (Figure 6.2f).

POINTS TO REMEMBER

- The gliding skate must glide straight backward on the flat of the blade, pointing along the line of travel. It should be situated under the hip of that leg. Because the gliding foot determines direction, you will go where it points. If both feet turn as you pivot and push, you will be forced to travel a snakelike S pattern which will slow you down considerably. The push-and-glide sequence of the backward stride is diagrammed in Figure 6.3.

- When thrusting the C-cut you should feel as though your inside edge is cutting into the ice. However, cut only until you are at full extension. The return phase is a glide. If you cut the ice as the skate returns you will slow yourself down.

- Keep the entire blade lengths of both skates in full contact with the ice. If you lift one or both heels off the ice your body will pitch over your toes.

- The knee of the thrusting leg snaps into the fully extended position at a point corresponding to the middle of the C. It must, however, be well bent and coiled under your body at the beginning and endpoints of the C, which correspond respectively to the coil and return points of the thrust.

- Keep your shoulders held back and your back straight (almost vertical). If you have to lean on your stick to prevent yourself from falling, you have either lifted your heels or leaned too far forward.

- Keep your head up and look straight ahead. Lowering your head causes your weight to be thrown forward and your body to lean over your toes, causing loss of balance and perhaps a fall.

- Keep your hips square (facing straight ahead) throughout the stride. You will travel wherever your hips are facing. If you turn

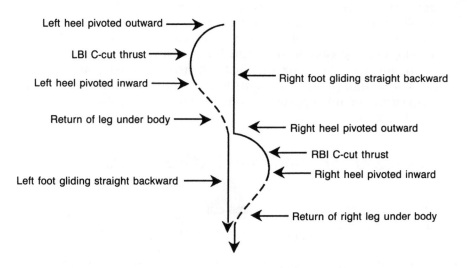

Figure 6.3   Pattern of the backward C-cut.

them sideways as you cut each C, you will waddle from side to side and lose speed.

- Hold the stick in your top hand only, the stick on the ice out in front of you, and use your arms in a diagonal forward-backward line and in rhythm with your legs (as in the forward stride). As your left leg pushes to the front and side, your left arm drives back; as your right leg pushes to the front and side, your right arm drives back.

- Try for full, rapid strides. At the full extension of each push your thrusting leg should be as far away from your body as it will reach, with that knee locked and the toe of the inside edge pushing against the ice. The toe flick provides the final thrust, just as it does in forward striding.

- Try to develop varying rhythms of striding backward (similar to forward striding). Remember that the tempo of each leg drive depends on how quickly you return the free leg. Again—all strides should be full strides!

The Glide of the Backward Stride

The glide of the backward stride is the reverse of the glide of the forward stride. Likewise, you don't actually glide a straight line, but a slightly curved line as in the forward stride (see chapter 5). Figure 6.4a diagrams the actual glide-and-push pattern of the backward stride. Figure 6.4b diagrams an incorrect pattern, caused by turning both feet the same way during the push. For learning purposes it is best to glide straight backward as described. Try to develop the ability to have the pushing leg and gliding leg work independently rather than together (i.e., both traveling the same way). One leg should glide a straight line while the other pushes and returns in a semicircular motion.

Exercises for Improving the Backward Stride

The following exercises, practiced conscientiously, should help you develop the skill, coordination, and power to become proficient at skating straight backward.

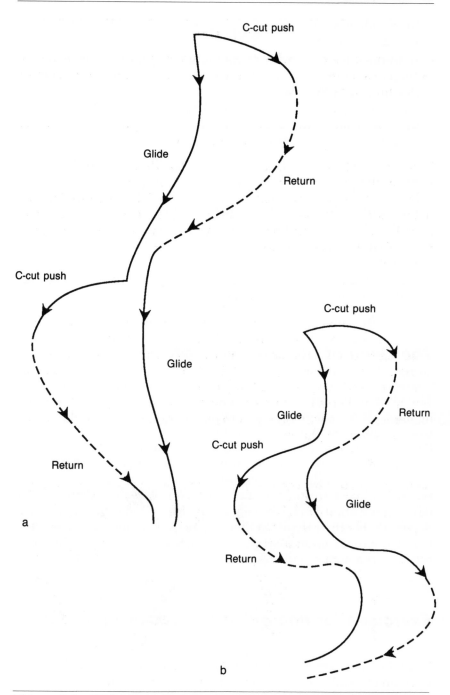

Figure 6.4   Glide of the backward stride: (a) correct; (b) incorrect.

Swizzles

Backward swizzles provide an elementary means for the learning skater to execute backward pushes. See chapter 3 for directions for performing this exercise.

Backward C-Cut

Perform a series of C-cuts as you skate straight backward. Concentrate on the pivot prior to each push, the proper use of the inside edge, leg drive, full extension, and return of the pushing leg to a point under your body weight before thrusting with the other leg. Be sure to keep the gliding foot pointing straight back throughout (see C-Cut exercise, chapter 5).

Resistance

Face another player and hold a stick between you. Holding on to the stick with one hand, use backward C-cut thrusts to pull the resisting skater across the ice (Figures 6.5a and b). You must travel straight backward with your gliding foot while making each C-cut push and returning the pushing leg under the body. The forward skater should do a two-foot snowplow stop (see chapter 9) to resist movement. This will force you to exaggerate the use of the inside edge and the leg thrusts.

b   a

Figure 6.5   Resistance exercise.

Hockey Stick Exercise

Use this exercise to train the gliding foot to travel in a straight line while the thrusting foot pivots, makes the C-cut push, and returns.

1. Place a hockey stick on the ice.
2. Stand on the left of the stick and next to it.
3. Place your gliding (right) foot close to the stick and parallel to it. Prepare to glide straight back on the flat of the blade in a direction parallel to the stick.
4. Pivot the heel of your pushing (left) foot outward (Figure 6.6a).
5. Execute one backward C-cut thrust with your left leg. Push to full extension and glide straight backward on your right skate, staying parallel and next to the stick (Figure 6.6b).
6. Continue to glide and return the left leg under your body until your heels touch each other (Figure 6.6c).
7. Stop.

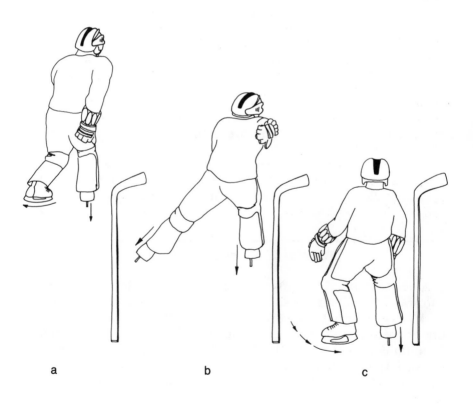

a   b   c

Figure 6.6   Hockey stick exercise.

8. Repeat the exercise on the right side of the stick. Now your left foot will be the gliding foot and your right foot the pushing foot. Cut one backward C-cut push with your right leg and glide straight backward on your left skate. After your right leg reaches full extension, return it under your body until your heels touch each other, and stop.

Keep repeating this procedure, alternating left and right C-cut pushes. Push each time from a complete standstill. Remember to keep your head up, back straight, and hips square to the line of travel.

One Leg Push

Do backward C-cut thrusts all the way across the ice, using only your right leg as the thrusting leg. Coming back across the ice do backward C-cut thrusts using only your left leg. Each push should be fully extended before returning. Next try using only four pushes to take you completely across the ice (six for smaller skaters). Each thrust should make you go faster than the previous thrust. Be sure your gliding foot always travels straight backward—don't zigzag.

The Return

To practice the return phase of the backward stride, repeat the previous four exercises, but on every return make the heel of the returning skate actually touch the heel of the gliding skate.

Forward Versus Defender

Practice with another player by competing as a defender against a forward. The defender should stand at the blue line and prepare to skate backward (Figure 6.7). The forward should stand at the goal line opposite from the defender and prepare to skate forward. Start simultaneously at a whistle signal. The object is for the defender to skate straight backward (no crossovers) and not allow the forward to catch and pass him or her. Alternate with your partner, taking turns as forward and defender.

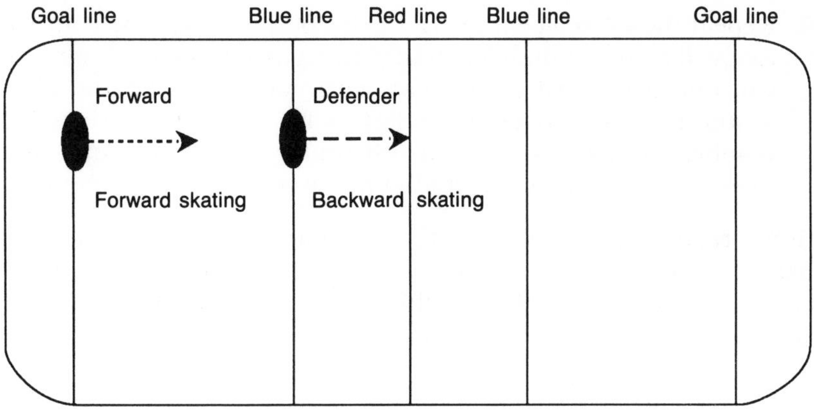

Figure 6.7   Forward versus defender.

CROSSOVERS

Crossovers are the moves used to skate corners or curves. They are the key to a player's lateral mobility. Watch the lyrical skating of such big leaguers as Paul Coffey and Denis Savard and you will see how effectively they execute crossovers. Crossovers are used for swerving in and out of traffic, weaving and zigzagging down the ice, and circling. They are also the means of gaining speed on curves. In short, crossover techniques are vital to a hockey player's maneuverability.

General characteristics of crossovers can be summarized as follows:

1. Forward and backward crossovers are very similar. Both should be mastered by all players.
2. "Crossover" refers to the passing of your outside foot (the one near the outside of the curve) over the toe of your inside foot (Figure 7.1).
3. When skating crossovers you always glide on strong edges, and your line of travel is always a curve. The manner in which your skates and body coordinate to produce edges for crossovers (Figure 7.2) is discussed in chapter 2.
4. On both forward and backward crossover maneuvers the inside foot *always* glides on its outside edge, while the outside foot *always* glides on its inside edge. The skates should lean into the curve at about 45-degree angles. The deeper the gliding edge, the sharper your curve.

Figure 7.1   Crossovers: Outside foot crosses over the toe of the inside foot.

Figure 7.2   Skates and body coordinate to produce edges for crossovers.

5. As in all other skating maneuvers, to achieve power you must use a wind-up, a release, a follow-through, and a return on every stride. Review the principles of edges, knee bend, body weight, weight shift, and glide, and apply them to crossovers as described in the following list.

   • Each thrust must start with the pushing foot centered under your body and end with the pushing leg fully extended away from your body.
   • Use strong edges to grip the ice with the pushing skate as well as with the gliding skate.
   • Bend your knees deeply and center your weight over the thrusting skate.
   • Keep the knee of the gliding leg well bent as the pushing leg thrusts to full extension and as the pushing leg returns.

- Return each pushing leg quickly to a position under your body weight to prepare for the next thrust. Keep the skate close to the ice as it returns.

6. Remember, a combination of powerful, complete leg drive and rapid leg movement produces speed. *One without the other is insufficient.*

Forward Crossovers

The instructions given are for skating on a counterclockwise circle (right-over-left crossovers). Your left leg will be the inside leg; your right leg will be the outside leg.

The First Push: The Stride Push

This push is essentially the same as the push of the forward stride and is executed by the outside leg.

1. Prepare to glide forward on the outside edge of your inside (left) skate (LFO) and to push with your outside (right) leg.
2. Place your weight over the outside (right) skate, bend your knees and dig in the inside edge so that the skate and lower leg form a 45-degree angle to the ice (the wind-up).
3. Push out and back (at about 45 degrees from your line of travel) directly against the entire length of the inside edge of the right skate (Figures 7.3a and b). Do not push the leg straight back (in a running motion). This causes a slip against the flat of the blade rather than a push against the edge.
4. Use the entire blade length to thrust. Start the push with the heel of the inside edge, shift your weight forward on the blade as you push, and complete the push with the "toe flick" from the front of the inside edge, as you would on the thrust of the forward skating stride.
5. At the midpoint of the push, transfer your weight from the inside edge of your right skate onto the LFO which takes the ice to glide (see Figure 7.3c). Keep the left knee well bent throughout the glide.
6. Thrust to full extension. At the end of the push the knee of your pushing leg (now the free leg) should be locked, with that foot held about one inch off the ice and the blade fairly parallel to the ice though the toe will be slightly closer than the heel to the ice (see Figure 7.3c). The knee of your gliding (left) leg stays well bent.

7. Immediately after the pushing (right) leg locks, return it quickly and begin crossing it over in front of the toe of the gliding (left) foot (see Figure 7.3d). Keep the skate close and parallel to the ice as it moves to cross over. It should take your weight and the ice on its right inside edge (RFI) at the midpoint of the second push (Figure 7.3e). Keep the right knee well bent as you glide.

a

b

c

d

e

f

Figure 7.3   Forward crossover sequence.

The Second Push: The Scissor (or Crossunder) Push

This push is executed by the inside leg. The scissor push gets its name from the scissoring action created by one leg crossing under the body to push while the other leg crosses over to take the ice and glide. Sometimes the push is called a "crossunder" push to emphasize the importance of this push from the inside leg. For youngsters I call it an X push.

Before your right foot takes the ice to glide on the RFI, your left leg must begin to push. Until now you have been gliding on the LFO.

1. Deepen the LFO by increasing the pressure against the outside of the boot (see Figure 7.3e).
2. Keep your weight over the LFO, bend your knees, and thrust your left leg sideways underneath your body, directly out and back against the entire length of the outside edge.
3. Start the push with the heel of the outside edge, shift your weight forward on the blade as you push, and complete the push with the "toe flick" from the front of the outside edge (Figure 7.3f). Do not push the leg straight back (in a running motion). This will cause a slip against the flat of the blade rather than a push against the edge. Avoid lifting your heel and pointing your toe down at the beginning of the push as the skater in Figure 7.4 is doing; the front tip of your skate (the flat of the blade) may catch the ice and your foot will slip backward, disengaging the outside edge, eliminating the thrust, and possibly causing a fall.
4. At the midpoint of the push, transfer your weight from the LFO onto the RFI, which now becomes the gliding skate.
5. Thrust until your left leg reaches full extension outside the circle, as demonstrated in Figure 7.3f. At the finish of the push,

Figure 7.4 Incorrect: Inside leg slips back.

the knee of your pushing (left) leg—now your free leg—should be locked, with the free foot held about one inch from and fairly parallel to the ice, though the toe will be slightly closer to the ice than the heel. The knee of your gliding foot should still (as always) be well bent.

6. Immediately after the pushing (left) leg locks, bring it quickly back to its return position under your body and next to the right foot. Keep the returning foot close to and almost parallel to the ice as it returns (Figure 7.5a). Lifting it high off the ice raises the center of gravity and delays the return process (Figure 7.5b).

a

b

Figure 7.5   The return of the inside leg after thrusting: (a) correct; (b) too high.

You have finished one sequence. Repeat the procedure, thrusting with your right leg against the inside edge of your right skate and gliding onto the LFO.

Skating Clockwise (Left Over Right)

Mirror the above procedure. Your right foot is now the inside foot, and your left foot is now the outside foot.

POINTS TO REMEMBER
(Forward Crossovers)

- When gliding on the outside edge of the inside foot, keep your weight on the back half of the blade. If your weight is too far forward the outside edge cannot cut into the ice; the skate will fishtail into a skid, causing you to lose your grip against the ice and your control. Hockey players often slide even when on a well-edged skate because their weight is too far forward on the blade. The tighter the curve, the more you must concentrate your weight on the back half of the blade.

- When quick acceleration is needed, run the first one or two crossover sequences. However, even when running the crossovers, *you must still thrust against the edges with full leg drive.* When running, keep your body weight low and project it toward the direction of travel. Jumping upward breaks the forward momentum.

Backward Crossovers

Backward crossovers are important to the maneuverability of all players but are especially critical in defensive situations. Defenders often use them in tracking an oncoming puck carrier. Players also use them to take opponents out of the play, as when a defender makes a backward-to-forward turn to cut off an attacking player. Defenders should start moving in such a way that they face the action. This requires them to start out rapidly while skating backward. Backward crossovers are the fastest and most effective way of accelerating backward.

When skated counterclockwise, the backward crossover is a left-over-right foot move. Your right foot is nearer the inside of the curve, and your left foot is nearer the outside. As in forward crossovers,

Figure 7.6   Backward crossover: left over right.

it is always the outside foot that crosses over in front of the toe of the inside foot (Figure 7.6) while the inside leg crosses under the body in the process of thrusting.

The instructions given are for skating a counterclockwise circle (left-over-right crossovers).

The First Push: The Stride Push

This push is essentially the C-cut thrust of the backward stride, except that on the return the thrusting foot crosses over in front of the gliding foot instead of centering under your body. It is executed by the outside leg.

1. Prepare to glide backward on the outside edge of your inside (right) skate (RBO), and to push with your outside (left) leg.
2. Place your weight over your outside (left) foot, bend your knees, and dig the inside edge into the ice so the skate and lower leg form a 45-degree angle to the ice (the wind-up).
3. Pivot your left heel outward (toward the outside of the circle) and execute a C-cut push against the inside edge of the left skate (Figure 7.7a). Thrust the left leg to the front and side (at a 45-degree angle to the line of travel), pushing directly against the entire length of the inside edge.
4. At the midpoint of the push, transfer your weight from the inside edge of your left skate to the RBO. Keep the right knee well bent throughout the glide (Figure 7.7b).
5. Thrust to full extension. At the end of the thrust the knee of your pushing leg (now the free leg) should be locked, with that foot held close to or on the ice.

6. Immediately after the left leg locks, return it quickly and begin crossing it over in front of the toe of your right foot. Keep it close to or on the ice as it moves to cross over (see Figure 7.7b). At the midpoint of the second push, transfer your weight to the LBI and glide. Keep your left knee well bent as you glide.

c

b

a

Figure 7.7 Backward crossover sequence (counterclockwise).

The Second Push: The Scissor (or Crossunder) Push

This push is executed by the inside leg and is identical to the scissor (crossunder) push of forward crossovers.

Before your left foot takes the ice to glide on its inside edge, your right (inside) leg, which until now has been gliding on its outside edge, must be activated to provide the second thrust. It is a requisite for power and for an effective crossover.

1. Deepen the RBO by increasing the pressure against the outside of the boot.
2. Keep your weight over the RBO, bend your knees, and thrust your right leg sideways underneath your body, directly forward and out against the entire outside edge (Figure 7.7c).
3. Start the push toward the back of the outside edge, shift your weight forward on the blade as you push, and complete the push with the "toe flick" from the front of the outside edge. Do not push the leg in a straight back (running) motion as this will cause a slip against the flat of the blade rather than a push against the edge.
4. At the midpoint of the push, transfer your weight from the RBO to the LBI, which takes the ice as the gliding skate.
5. Keep thrusting with your right leg until the leg reaches full extension outside the circle, as demonstrated in Figure 7.7c. At the end of the thrust the knee of your pushing (right) leg, now your free leg, should be locked, with that foot held close and almost parallel to the ice. The knee of your gliding leg should remain well bent.
6. Immediately after your right leg locks, bring it quickly back to its return position under your body and next to the left foot. Keep it close and almost parallel to the ice as it returns.

You have finished one sequence. Repeat the procedure, pivoting your left foot outward to execute the C-cut push against the inside edge of your left skate and gliding on the RBO.

Skating Clockwise (Right Over Left)

Mirror the procedure just described. Your left foot is now the inside foot, and your right foot the outside one (Figures 7.8a, b, and c).

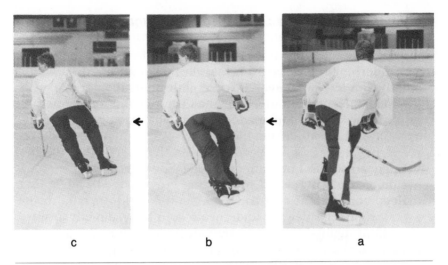

c   b   a

Figure 7.8 Backward crossover sequence (clockwise).

POINTS TO REMEMBER
(Forward and Backward Crossovers)

- The crossover sequence includes two thrusts—the first from the inside blade edge of the outside skate, the second from the outside blade edge of the inside skate. If one is neglected, you will lose half your power.

- The depth of the edges you should apply to the ice is directly related to the sharpness of the curve you are skating, as well as to your speed. You can use shallower edges when weaving down the ice in a shallow S curve than you can when making a sharp turn. Also, when traveling fast you can use deeper edges than when you are traveling slowly. Develop the ability to adjust the depth of your edges to the situation at hand: Sharper curves and/or greater speed require greater lean of edges and knees.

- The manner in which the skate and body coordinate to produce curves, as explained in chapter 2, should be carefully reviewed.

- Only one foot performs the actual crossover maneuver. It is always the outside foot, crossing over in front of the toe of the inside foot.
- The quality of the scissor (crossunder) push affects the quality of the crossover maneuver. If you cross under only partially you will not only eliminate the follow-through and subsequently inhibit your power and speed, but you will also produce an inadequate crossover. When the crossover/crossunder is executed properly your legs will be crossed from the tops of your thighs, not just from your knees and feet. The ability of goalies to cross over is especially related to a strong crossunder because this makes room for their pads.
- After each thrust and during each return, keep the free foot close and almost parallel to the ice. You should feel as if you are dragging your foot on the ice as it returns. Kicking up the heels or lifting your foot up high may be caused by bending the knee of the free leg during the return. This delays the return process and raises your center of gravity.
- When performing the actual crossover, keep your feet parallel to each other and to the line of travel. If either foot turns at an angle different from the line of travel, your line of travel will change.

POINTS TO REMEMBER
(Backward Crossovers)

- To achieve a more complete backward C-cut thrust, do the following: As you start the C-cut, push with your outside foot, and while your inside foot is still off the ice, reach your inside foot sideways into the circle. When the inside foot takes the ice your feet will be separated by a distance somewhat wider than the width of your shoulders (Figure 7.9a). This allows your outside foot to achieve a more complete C-cut thrust.
- Execute the backward crossunder push as if you were scooping the circle under you with the inside foot and leg (Figure 7.9b).
- Drive your inside leg well underneath your body before attempting to cross the outside leg over. If you don't it may get in the

way of your outside leg as it crosses and your feet may trip each other.

- Keep your weight toward the front halves of the blades.
- Keep your hips and feet facing directly backward over your line of travel. There is a tendency to turn your hips sideways as you cut the C, which will force you to skate sideways instead of backward.
- Good posture is critical to the proper execution of backward crossovers. If you lean too far forward your weight will pitch over the toes of your blades and you will lose your balance. If you are forced to use your stick as a "third leg," it means your body weight is not centered over the front halves of your blades as it should be.

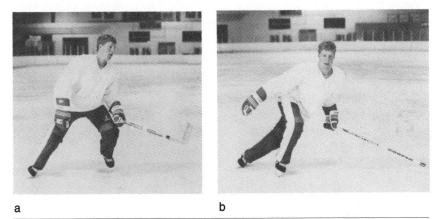

a   b

Figure 7.9   (a) Inside foot reaches into the circle; (b) inside foot and leg scoop circle under the body.

Backward crossovers differ from forward crossovers in the following ways:

- As in all backward skating, your weight should be over the front halves of the blades.
- When executing right-over-left backward crossovers you will travel a clockwise curve. The inside foot is your left foot, and the outside foot is your right foot. Left-over-right crossovers are just the opposite.
- The push from the inside edge (outside leg) is the C-cut push (as in straight backward skating), the thrust should be to the front and side to full extension.
- The returning (free) foot may actually stay in slight contact with the ice rather than leaving the ice.

Body Positioning and Control in Crossovers

Your ability to maneuver while skating on a curve or circle is largely affected by the position and control of your upper body. Your body must be positioned so that your hips and skates face the direction of travel. Your shoulders should remain still and level, which requires considerable practice. Excessive arm, chest, and shoulder movement compromises your balance, your ability to push correctly, and your ability to stickhandle. If you tilt your upper body into the circle by dropping your inside shoulder too much you can easily fall or be knocked down.

Two upper body positions may be used when performing forward crossovers. Both should be mastered: (a) Position your upper body so that your chest and shoulders face toward the center of the curve (Figure 7.10a); (b) Position your upper body so that your chest and shoulders face toward the outside of the curve (Figure 7.10b). Note that in both positions your upper body is twisted at the waist rather than at the hips, which face the direction of travel. The upper body position for backward crossovers is usually position a (facing into the curve).

a   b

Figure 7.10   Body positions for forward crossovers: Upper body faces (a) toward center of curve; (b) away from center of curve.

Practice crossovers holding the hockey stick in both hands, the stick on the ice in its position for stickhandling. Practice both body positions skating forward, and position a skating backward. Do the same thing holding the stick in just your top hand. Do not let your arms, chest, and shoulders move as you skate the crossovers.

Exercises for Improving Forward and Backward Crossovers

The exercises in this section emphasize

- proper use of the edges;
- development of power in both leg thrusts; and
- correct body position and control.

When crossover exercises are practiced, clockwise and counterclockwise directions should be emphasized equally.

Walking Crossovers (Sidestepping)

Stand facing the endboards of the rink. Walk sideways across the ice to the opposite side. Walk to the left, crossing the right foot over the left. The right (outside or trailing) foot will push against its inside edge, as in a stride push, as the left (inside or leading) skate steps onto its outside edge. After the right leg pushes it will cross over in front of the left foot and step onto its inside edge as the left leg crosses under the body to push as in a scissor push. Keep your skates pointing at the endboards. Walk in this manner from one set of sideboards to the other. Practice this exercise in both directions. This is an effective way to learn the basic steps of the crossover sequence, both forward and backward. When doing this exercise your feet should be parallel to each other at all times.

Variation:

Do the same drill, stretching the legs sideways to full extension to develop the feeling of both the direction and extension of the leg drive from the stride and scissor pushes.

Outside Edge Scissor Cuts

This exercise emphasizes the outside edge thrusts. Both your gliding foot and your thrusting foot must be on outside edges at all times. Note the scissoring action of the legs as one crosses under to push and the other crosses over to glide.

1. Skate forward on the LFO, right foot off the ice. You will curve in a counterclockwise direction (Figure 7.11a).

2. Begin to cross the right foot over the left.
3. Thrust the left leg against its outside edge as the right foot crosses over. Thrust it sideways underneath you as far as it will go. The right foot, after crossing over, will take the ice on its RFO and glide a clockwise curve (Figure 7.11b).
4. Lift your left skate off the ice (Figure 7.11c). Uncross it and bring it alongside your right foot in preparation for crossing it in front of your right skate (Figure 7.11d). As your left foot uncrosses and moves forward, keep it near and fairly parallel to the ice.

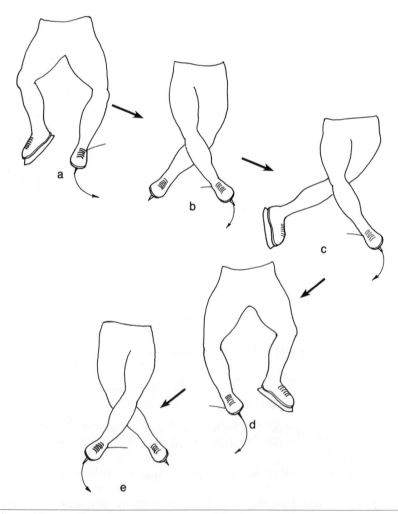

Figure 7.11   Outside edge scissor cuts, alternating feet.

5. Prepare to push with the right leg as the left foot moves forward.
6. Thrust the right leg against the outside edge as the left foot crosses over. Thrust it sideways underneath you as far as it will go. The left foot, after crossing over, will take the ice on its LFO and glide a counterclockwise curve (Figure 7.11e).
7. You have completed one sequence. Keep repeating the sequence, continuously crossing over and scissor-thrusting.
8. Perform the exercise skating backward (Figures 7.11e, d, c, b, a).

POINTS TO REMEMBER

- Be sure you are gliding on and pushing from outside edges.
- Push against the entire blade length.
- Start this exercise slowly. Try to accelerate with each successive thrust. If you merely maintain your speed with each thrust rather than increase it, you are not thrusting with optimum power. When you reach top speed, come to a complete stop and begin the exercise again, starting slowly.

S Curves

This exercise involves executing a series of S curves. It is performed on one skate at a time. It is an excellent exercise for improving inside and outside edges, both of which are essential for skating tight curves. It is also excellent for developing balance, knee bend, and quadricep strength.

The S curves are created by making a small semicircle skating on the RFO (clockwise) and then a small semicircle skating on the RFI (counterclockwise), and repeating the sequence continuously (Figure 7.12).

1. Glide on a deep RFO using a 45-degree angle of the skate and lower leg to the ice. Keep your left foot off the ice, next to your right foot.
2. Bend your skating knee deeply, flip your right ankle inward, and shift your weight so the skate is now on its inside edge, thereby changing the outside-edge lean to an inside-edge lean (also at 45 degrees). You will now be skating on the RFI.

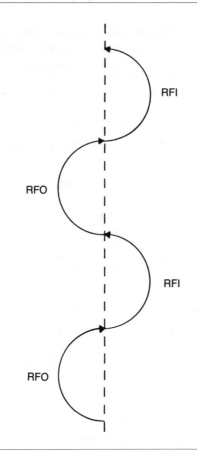

Figure 7.12 Forward S curves on right foot: An imaginary axis divides the outside edge curve from the inside edge curve.

3. While curving on the RFI, slightly straighten your right knee to release your weight. Then, to change to the right outside edge, bend your knee deeply while flipping your ankle outward and shifting your weight. You will once again be skating on the RFO.
4. See how many S curves you can execute before putting your left foot down. Try to skate the entire length of the ice on the same foot using the edges and knees to accelerate you.
5. Repeat the exercise on your left foot, skating forward.
6. Repeat the exercise skating backward on each foot. Only one foot should be on the ice for each entire set of S curves, and the depth of each curve should be the same. There is usually a tendency to make the curve deeper on the inside edge than on the outside edge. Concentrate on creating a deep outside

edge, since it requires greater control to execute this edge well. Strong edge angles and a strong rise and fall of the skating knee are needed to perform this exercise properly.

NOTE: Your weight must be on the back half of the blade to perform this move forward and the front half to perform it backward.

Resistance Crossovers

The purpose of this exercise is to develop more powerful leg drive in the forward and backward crossover moves. You will push a resisting player while executing crossovers.

Stand sideways to another player, holding a stick horizontally at chest height between you. The resisting player will face you. Prepare to push the other player.

Move the resisting player by doing crossovers. The player should try to prevent you from moving readily by doing a two-foot backward snowplow stop (see chapter 9).

a

b

c
d

Figure 7.13 Resistance crossovers.

To move the resisting player you will be forced to dig in your edges and thrust powerfully with your legs. You will actually be sidestepping across the ice. The leading foot corresponds to the inside leg on crossovers; it steps onto and thrusts against its outside edge. The trailing foot corresponds to the outside leg; it thrusts against its inside edge, crosses over in front of the toe of the inside leg, and steps onto its inside edge.

Thrust to full extension on every push. Keep head up and shoulders back as you push your partner across the ice. Push the resisting player all the way across the ice doing right-over-left crossovers (Figures 7.13a, b, c, and d). Coming back, use left-over-right crossovers to push the player. Both sides must be practiced equally.

Crossovers on a Circle

When learning to skate crossovers on a circle it is good practice to hold the stick with both hands and to keep the stick on the ice as if you were controlling the puck. This is a good way to practice keeping your shoulders still, which is necessary for puck control. As you gain upper body control, practice holding the stick with just your top hand. Practice all forward crossover exercises using both upper body positions: chest facing into the center of the circle and away from the center. When skating backward crossovers keep your chest facing toward the center of the circle. Finally, perform all crossover exercises skating backward as well as forward.

C-Cuts on a Circle

1. Skate a face-off circle in a clockwise direction. Thrust continuously with only the outside (left) leg; the inside skate should continuously glide on its outside edge. With the inside edge of the outside skate execute consecutive C-cuts around the circle (Figure 7.14). This exercise improves the outside leg thrust of the crossover sequence while training the inside skate to glide on an outside edge.
2. Repeat the exercise, skating around the face-off circle in a counterclockwise direction.

Consecutive Crossovers

Skate consecutive crossovers on a face-off circle. More advanced skaters should use deep edges to make the circle as small as possible, and try to stay within the face-off circle while skating fast.

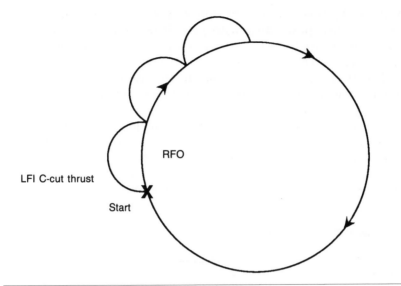

Figure 7.14   Forward C-cuts on a circle: clockwise direction.

Be careful not to let your upper body tilt into the circle by dropping your inside shoulder.

NOTE: When skating in the direction that has you hold the hockey stick on your backhand side (arm across your body), it is difficult to eliminate all tilt of the shoulders into the circle. Try to minimize it.

Vary this exercise by skating the circle three times using forward crossovers, then turning backward and skating the circle three times using backward crossovers.

Freeze

Perform consecutive crossovers on a face-off circle, skating fast. On a whistle signal, "freeze" so that you are balanced on whichever edge you happen to be gliding on when the whistle is blown; keep the other foot off the ice. See how long you can balance (freeze your weight) on that edge without putting the other foot down. Do this on both outside and inside edges, in both directions, using forward and backward crossovers. This is a test of how good your balance is on each edge at any given moment.

Five-Circle Crossovers

Start from one corner of the rink. Skate the nearest face-off circle three times, using crossovers (forward or backward). Then skate to the the next face-off circle, and skate crossovers on it three times in the other direction. Skate to the next circle, and skate it three times the original way. Execute the exercise using all five face-off circles (Figure 7.15).

Be sure to alternate the direction to work on crossovers in both directions. Pay attention to improving the more difficult direction. Concentrate on technique. Go slowly at first, and think about what you're doing; as the maneuvers improve, accelerate the pace until you can perform correct technique at increasingly faster speeds.

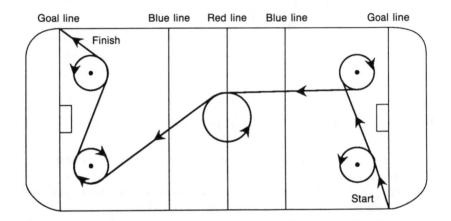

Figure 7.15　Five-circle crossovers.

Variations on Crossover Exercises

There are numerous variations on crossover exercises. These are just a sampling and can be expanded, changed, or elaborated upon.

Crossovers in Figure-Eight Patterns

1. Skate consecutive crossovers on a circle, clockwise. After skating the circle twice, skate to a second, tangent circle and skate it twice, counterclockwise. Then skate to the original circle and skate crossovers clockwise. Keep repeating.
2. Skate forward crossovers on a circle two times, then skate to the second circle and do backward crossovers two times around. Return to the original circle and skate forward crossovers two times around. Keep repeating.

Crossovers on the Same Circle

1. Skate crossovers on a face-off circle, clockwise. At the blowing of a whistle, stop, change direction, and skate crossovers on the same circle, counterclockwise.
2. Skate forward crossovers two times on a face-off circle, then turn and skate backward crossovers two times on the same circle. Be sure to practice both directions.

Two-Foot Crossovers

When performing this exercise you will skate forward crossovers on a circle. However, you must keep the heels of both skates *on the ice* all the time. The edges used for gliding and pushing are the same as in regular crossovers, but both pushes (the push from the outside leg and the push from the inside leg) are executed solely with the back halves of the blades. *The toes are not used.* The directions given apply to skating a counterclockwise circle.

1. Push with your outside (right) leg by doing a forward C-cut thrust, pushing against the inside edge to full extension (Figure 7.16a). Push with the back half of the blade and keep your right heel on the ice at full extension.
2. During the push, shift your weight onto the LFO and glide on it.
3. After your right leg reaches full extension, keep the right heel on the ice as you cross the right foot over in front of the toe of your left foot.
4. Thrust the inside (left) leg against its outside edge (crossing it

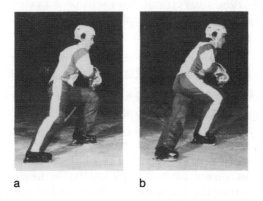

a   b

Figure 7.16 Two-foot crossovers.

under your body; Figure 7.16b). Push with the back half of the blade and keep your left heel on the ice as the leg pushes.

5. During the push, shift your weight onto the RFI and glide on it.
6. After the left leg reaches full extension under your body, keep the left heel on the ice and glide the left skate back to a position alongside your right foot. You have completed one sequence.

Keep repeating the sequence on the circle. Then mirror the above instructions and practice it skating a clockwise circle. The exercise can also be done using backward crossovers, but because of its difficulty that is recommended for more advanced skaters.

The Two-Foot Crossover above exercise develops many of the skills needed for effective crossover strides:

• Keeping a strong knee bend on the gliding foot during the actual crossover move
• Having your body weight on the pushing leg for an effective push
• Using the back of the blade to initiate each push before completing each push with the toe
• Developing powerful leg drive
• Developing full extension
• Training the return leg to stay close and parallel to the ice as it moves back to its original position.

Body Control Exercises

These exercises stress correct upper body position and control. If you position your upper body properly and control excessive arm, shoulder, and chest movement, you will be a better balanced and stronger skater. Some professional hockey players compensate for a lack of exceptional speed with superb control.

Crossovers: Chest Facing Into the Circle

Skate the following exercises with your chest facing the center of the circle. The object is to train the upper body to remain still while performing crossovers.

1. Skate crossovers on a circle. Hold the hockey stick with both hands, keeping the stick on the ice. If your chest is positioned properly the stick will ride inside the circle and the tip of the stick blade will point toward the face-off dot at the center of

the circle. This should be the case on both your forehand and backhand sides.

Do not let the stick move around. If you can keep the stick in the same position as you skate, this indicates that your arms, chest, and shoulders are under control. Remember, if you move your arms, chest, and shoulders when stickhandling the puck you will move the stick and will lose the puck as a result. It is critical to learn to skate with your upper body still.

2. Skate crossovers with your hockey gloves balanced atop your outstretched hands. This requires you to keep arms, chest, and shoulders still; if you move them, the gloves will fall.

3. Skate crossovers holding a cup of water in each outstretched hand. Try not to spill the water. This requires you to hold your upper body, arms and hands extremely still.

4. Skate crossovers with your hands clasped behind your back, or with your hands on your hips. This prevents arm, chest, and shoulder movement.

5. In this exercise a group of about six players skates forward crossovers around the same circle, counterclockwise. First, however, the players form a circle by having each player extend the right arm out front holding the handle of his or her stick, and extending the left arm behind to grasp the stick blade of the player behind. The players' chests should face the center of the circle. Skate forward crossovers around the circle.

6. Do the same thing skating backward crossovers. The circular direction will now be clockwise. To do forward or backward crossovers in the opposite direction, players must extend their left arms out front and their right arms behind.

Linking up in this manner locks the shoulders and chest in the desired positions. This exercise helps to improve the ability to keep your upper body in the correct position when skating crossovers.

7. Practice crossovers by yourself in this body position, holding the stick with just your top hand and keeping the stick in its proper place on the ice as you skate. Do not let it move around.

Crossovers: Chest Facing Outside the Circle

This body position is often needed when you are trying to swerve around a defending player. As you push your opponent away with your inside arm and shoulder, your chest should face out of the curve. In some game situations you often hold the stick with just your top hand.

Skate these exercises with your back always facing the center of the circle. Again, the idea is to train the upper body to remain still and correctly positioned while you perform crossovers.

1. Skate forward crossovers on a circle, chest facing away from the circle. Your back will face the center of the circle. Hold the stick with both hands, keeping the stick on the ice. In this exercise the stick will be outside the circle. Keep the stick still (in the same position) as you skate the circles.
2. Perform steps 2, 3, and 4 from the previous set of exercises (Crossovers: Chest Facing Into the Circle) with your chest facing outside the circle.
3. Have a group of players link up around a circle as in step 5 of the previous exercise, but now hold the sticks so that chests face outside the circle. To skate forward crossovers around a counterclockwise circle, the left hand will extend to hold the handle of the stick in front, and the right hand will extend to hold the stick blade of the person in back. Again, the goal is to lock the shoulders and chests into their proper positions, to experience the correct upper body position, and to eliminate excess arm, chest, and shoulder movement.
4. Practice forward crossovers using this upper body position, now holding the hockey stick with only your top hand. Again, keep the stick in its proper place on the ice as you skate. Don't let it move around.

Running Crossovers

For sudden acceleration in hockey, players take a few running or leaping steps. Running steps are very effective for accelerating quickly, but once speed is built up you should no longer run. For maximum speed with greatest efficiency the glide of the skate must be taken advantage of. Skaters who constantly "run" often tire prematurely.

Practice running crossovers by sprinting on the edges. Don't forget to use the full thrusting action of your legs even when running, and leap outward, not upward (Figure 7.17).

NOTE: When running, the body weight should be on the fronts of the edges (from the ball of the foot to the toe) similar to when starting (see chapter 8).

To perform the exercise, skate crossovers on a circle at a slow pace. On a whistle signal, run the crossovers, accelerating with powerful, rapid, and fully extended thrusts. On the next whistle, slow down, and on the next, run again. Do the exercise both forward and backward.

Figure 7.17   Running crossovers.

Weaving Crossovers

Weaving is accomplished by crossing over one way (right over left) and then alternating to cross over the other way (left over right). In weaving crossovers, a third step is added to the crossover sequence to neutralize the original direction of curve and body weight so that you can change to the new direction. It is a sequence of three steps instead of two. To gain speed you must thrust onto the third step rather than simply stepping onto it. The third step is skated on the foot that was the inside foot (outside edge) in the crossover move, but on its *inside edge* instead. The third thrust is executed by the same leg that executed the first one. The thrust is from the inside edge of the blade, and is otherwise identical to the first thrust.

NOTE: Whereas the power base for straight forward or straight backward skating is centered under the midline of the body, the power for lateral mobility comes from a wide base. In order to shift weight rapidly from side to side the feet should be somewhat wider apart than the shoulders. Therefore the third step is best executed as a wide step, planted on a strong inside edge with the body weight totally committed over the planted foot. This prepares the player for a quick transition from one direction to another. (Figures 7.18a-i show weaving forward crossovers. Figures 7.19a-i show weaving backward crossovers. Figure 7.20 diagrams the pattern of weaving backward crossovers.)

1. Practice weaving crossovers around pylons. Develop the ability to skate a tight S curve pattern (Figure 7.21a).

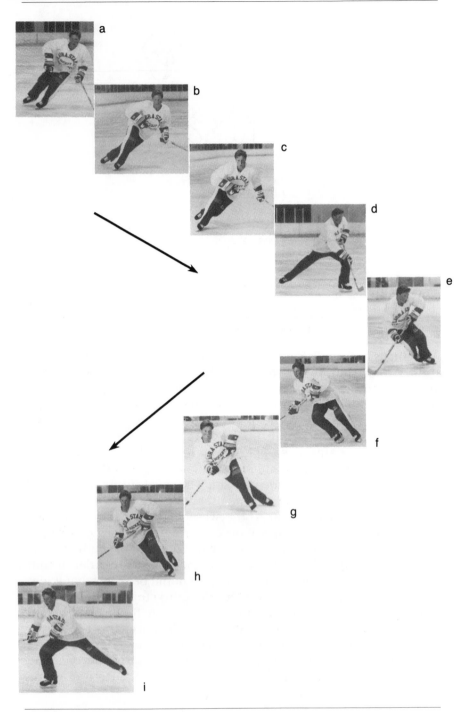

Figure 7.18   Weaving forward crossover sequence.

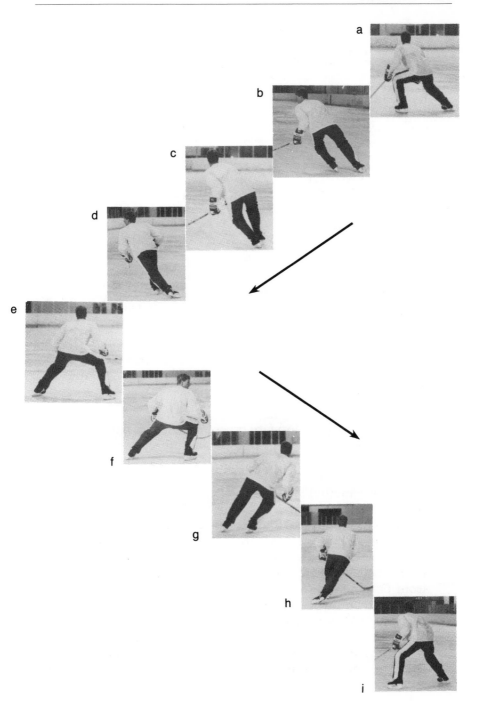

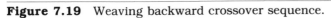

Figure 7.19   Weaving backward crossover sequence.

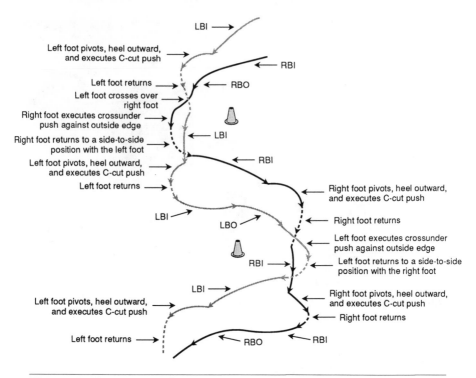

Figure 7.20   Pattern of weaving backward crossovers.

2. Vary the drill. Skate forward crossovers in an S pattern around two pylons. Then turn around and do the same thing skating backward crossovers. Figure 7.21b shows a slightly different, more difficult course.

3. Work with another skater, one of you skating as a forward and the other as a defender. The forward, skating with a puck, should start at the goal line and skate forward crossovers weaving a zigzag pattern down the ice. The defender should start at the first blue line and track the forward, skating a zigzag pattern of backward crossovers and trying to prevent the forward from passing him or her.

4. Zigzag down the ice. Skate two crossovers right over left, and then alternate and do two left over right. You can also do them singly or by threes. Do the exercise skating forward and backward. Practice stepping out wide and onto the inside edge on the third (neutralizing) step of every sequence.

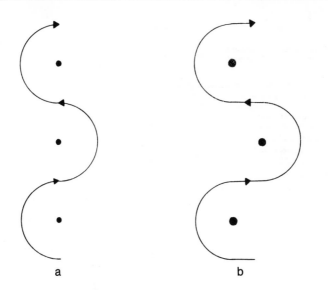

a   b

Figure 7.21   Weaving crossovers around pylons: alternating the direction of crossovers.

Chapter

8

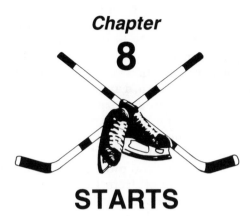

STARTS

Hockey games can be won or lost in fractions of a second. It is often the first few steps that determine who gets the advantage. Players who don't start out quickly can find themselves hopelessly behind the play. You *must* develop the ability to move quickly into high gear from a complete stop. Players should be able to accelerate explosively from any position.

Explosive starts require quick, running-type strides: strides so rapid they appear choppy, since the skates do not have time to glide. They are, however, accompanied by extremely powerful, complete, and rapid leg drives. The techniques of starting on ice are similar to those of a sprinter leaving the starting block, striving to achieve as much quickness, power, and distance as possible on every thrust.

There are three requisites to achieving explosive acceleration. The most critical of these is quickness—quick feet, or rapid leg turnover. To accomplish this the skater must "run" the initial strides on the the toes of the skates (the fronts of the inside edges). The purpose is to use the skates in a "touch and go" technique to quicken the leg movement. If the entire blade length is in contact with the ice, the skate may glide. This delays the next stride.

The second requisite is power. Power is derived from the force exerted by the legs and body weight driving directly against the

gripping edge. Full leg drive and total leg recovery are as imperative when starting as when striding. Nothing can propel you forward unless the legs drive fully in the opposite direction.

The third requirement is to project your weight in the desired
direction of travel as you push. The distance covered in the starting strides is related to the forward angle of the upper body. A strong
forward angle of the trunk produces greater distance. Because the
skating (contact) foot must take the ice under the center of gravity
(chest) the further the chest is extended, the further forward the
foot must step in order to maintain balance. In other words, while
running the first few strides, you must throw your weight outward
similar to a sprinter taking off from the starting block.

There are three basic starts: forward, side (crossover), and backward. As in every aspect of skating, the secrets of good starts include (a) the proper use of the edges to provide grip into the ice,
(b) proper distribution of body weight, and (c) optimum leg thrust.
As always, the principles of wind-up, release, follow-through, and
return apply. By developing the three basic starts, you can get an
efficient takeoff no matter which way you are facing when you stop,
and no matter which way you want to go when you start out again.

Forward (Front) Start

A forward start is used when you are facing straight ahead. This
occurs, for example, after you have skated backward and stopped,
then want to proceed forward again; or when, after a face-off, play
demands that you accelerate straight ahead from your position.

The First Stride

1. Pivot both feet outward to form an exaggerated letter V with
   heels together and toes apart. Each foot should be turned outward at an angle approximately 80 degrees from the forward
   line of travel (Figures 8.1 and 8.2a).
2. Center your weight over the pushing (right) leg (Figure 8.2b).
3. Bend your knees deeply (out ahead of the toes) and dig the inside edge of your right skate into the ice so that the skate and
   lower leg form an angle to the ice of approximately 45 degrees.
   The stronger the pressure into the ice of edge, knee bend, and
   body weight (the wind-up), the more power available for the
   thrust.

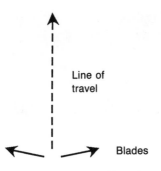

Figure 8.1   Forward (front) start: feet pivoted outward about 80 degrees from line of travel.

4. Shift your body weight strongly forward as you push with your right leg. To accelerate quickly your body weight must be low, angled well forward, and propelled powerfully by the thrusting leg, which pushes directly against the cutting edge (Figure 8.2c). Because your body weight is well forward, the primary thrust will be executed with the front portion of the inside edge. As you shift your weight, reach forward with the front (left) knee and foot. Keep moving the front foot forward until it makes contact with the ice under your chest (center of gravity) (Figures 8.2d and e). The powerful thrust and the forward angle of your body, front knee, and foot produces acceleration.

5. When the front (left) skate takes the ice, it should touch down on a strong inside edge (45-degree edge angle) with the skate turned outward approximately 70 degrees from the forward line of travel and with your body weight centered over the edge. Because of the strong forward inclination of your body, your weight will be on the front 2 to 3 inches of the inside edge. The heel of the blade should *not* touch the ice. When the front (left) foot touches down properly—gripping the ice strongly with the inside edge—it is immediately prepared to push (see Figure 8.2e). If it does not touch down on a strong enough edge, or if your weight is on the heel of the blade, you are forced to glide, causing a delay of the next stride.

6. After thrusting, the right leg (now the free leg) must immediately return, pass by the contact foot in a V position and reach forward to become the new contact foot. Keep the returning knee and foot turned outward as the leg returns, passes the contact foot, and moves forward to take the ice (Figure 8.2f).

a

b

c

d

e

f

g

Figure 8.2   Forward (front) start sequence.

The Second Stride

The left foot has taken the ice on the inside edge of the blade, with your body weight centered over it, knee well bent. As the front (left) foot contacts the ice it becomes the new pushing foot. The strong landing edge is immediately used as the pushing edge.

1. Thrust powerfully, pushing directly against the inside edge. Keep your body low and angled well forward. Push to full extension. As you push, shift your weight forward and reach forward with the right knee and foot, moving the foot forward until it makes contact with the ice under your chest (center of gravity) (Figure 8.2g).
2. When the right foot takes the ice, it should touch down on a strong inside edge (45-degree edge angle) with the skate still turned outward and your body weight centered over the edge. On this second stride the skate turnout should be about 60 degrees from the forward line of travel. Again, because of the strong forward inclination of the body, your weight will be on the front 2 to 3 inches of the inside edge. If your weight is on the heel of the blade you will be forced to glide, causing a delay of the next stride.
3. After thrusting, the left leg (now the free leg) must immediately return, pass by the contact foot in the V position, and reach forward to become the new contact foot. Keep the returning knee and foot turned outward as the leg returns, passes the contact foot, and moves forward to take the ice.

Subsequent Strides

You have completed the first two running steps of the start. Some players take three running steps. However, on the third or fourth step your movements should become similar to those used for the forward stride. In other words, you begin to take advantage of the glide of the skate. Continue to move your legs in a rapid sprinting motion. The angle of your upper body to the ice should gradually become more upright. On the sixth or seventh stride it should be in the forward stride position, inclined approximately 45 degrees to the ice. If your body becomes upright too suddenly, forward motion is impaired. Many of the fastest accelerating players use a strongly inclined body angle and maintain it longer than skaters who start less explosively.

POINTS TO REMEMBER

- Keep body weight inclined well forward.
- It takes a number of strides to build up speed. Use powerful, sprinting leg motions. Push to full extension on every stride.
- Recover each returning leg completely. The heels return and pass each other in the V position.
- Each rapid running stride should take you farther than the preceding one did. On the first step you are limited in the distance you can travel because your body is not yet in motion (you are overcoming inertia).
- Sprint *forward*—do not jump up! Your height off the ice should be minimal. Leap outward!
- The function of the edges is to form a solid wedge in the ice against which you vault yourself forward.
- Drive your arms in a forward-backward motion, in rhythm and on the same line of force with your legs. Do not swing your arms from side to side.
- Keep your head and chin up.
- The cuts your edges make in the ice as the skates touch down should be short, well turned out, and deep. These indicate that force has been successfully concentrated over a very short distance (no longer than the length of the blade) allowing for explosiveness. Gliding strides on the initial strides of the start, which show as long marks in the ice, dissipate force and take longer, causing leg speed to be slower. Figure 8.3 diagrams the initial strides of an explosive front start.

Figures 8.4a, b, and c show incorrect marks your skates may trace in the ice when you start. Note them and understand the mistakes that may cause them.

The marks shown in Figure 8.4a indicate a short, well turned cut. At some point during the push, however, the toe turned to point straight down and the leg slipped back on the flat of the blade. Result: no push, and loss of balance.

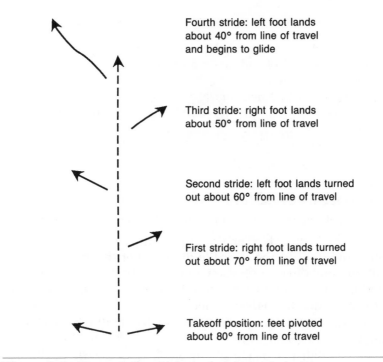

Fourth stride: left foot lands
about 40° from line of travel
and begins to glide

Third stride: right foot lands
about 50° from line of travel

Second stride: left foot lands turned
out about 60° from line of travel

First stride: right foot lands turned
out about 70° from line of travel

Takeoff position: feet pivoted
about 80° from line of travel

Figure 8.3   Forward (front) start, showing cuts in ice.

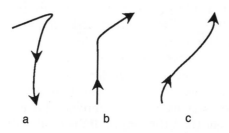

a   b   c

Figure 8.4   Common errors on initial strides of forward start: (a) toe
turned straight down; (b) blade contacted ice facing straight forward;
(c) heel of blade contacted ice.

The marks shown in Figure 8.4b indicate the skate blade made
contact with the ice facing straight forward. This caused a glide.
To push it was necessary to pivot the skate. Result: loss of valuable time.

The marks shown in Figure 8.4c indicate the heel of the blade
made contact with the ice. This caused a glide and, again, a slower
start.

Gliding may result from a variety of errors, such as

- insufficient edge on the touchdown,
- weight on the heel of the blade on touchdown,
- insufficient knee bend,
- body weight not inclined forward enough,
- contact foot facing forward on touchdown rather than turned outward, or
- slow leg recovery.

Side (Crossover) Start

A side (crossover) start is often used following a hockey stop, either to launch an attack in the opposite direction or to continue in the same direction. When the hockey stop is completed the player is turned sideways, ready to drive into the side start. When executed correctly the side start is very effective.

The side start is a crossover move in which the outside leg pushes first (against its inside edge) and the inside leg pushes second (against its outside edge). The inside (leading) leg drives under the body as the outside (trailing) foot crosses over the front foot and lands on its inside edge (Figure 8.5). As in the front start, the body weight must be projected low and outward (to the side). Shift it as if you were pushing a heavy weight with your shoulder. The initial steps should be taken as rapid, powerful running steps. As with the front start, the combination of quick feet, powerful leg drive, and distance covered yields an explosive start.

The side start maneuver is done as if you were leaping sideways along a line, crossing over as you move, your feet and body sideways to the intended line of travel (Figure 8.6). This is critical. If

Figure 8.5 Crossover start, right over left.

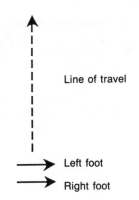

Line of travel

Left foot

Right foot

Figure 8.6   Side (crossover) start: feet perpendicular to the line of travel.

one or both feet turn forward to face the line of travel, the skates will glide forward rather than grip the ice, and it will be impossible to perform the crossover maneuver properly.

The following instructions describe a start to the left. To start to the right, reverse the feet and go in the opposite direction.

The First Stride

1. Your left foot will be your inside (leading) foot. Both feet must be at a right angle to your intended line of travel, shoulder width apart, knees bent (Figure 8.7a). Place your weight over the outside foot.
2. Push with the outside (right) leg and during the push, shift your weight sideways onto the left outside edge, driving your body weight to the left (Figure 8.7b).
3. Do a leaping right-over-left crossover. The inside (left) leg must thrust against its outside edge, pushing under your body to full extension. This is done as the outside (right) leg crosses over the left foot (Figures 8.7c and d). The right skate should land on the front 2 to 3 inches of its inside edge, turned approximately 70 degrees from the line of travel, your body weight centered over the edge (Figure 8.7e). The heel of the blade should not touch the ice.
4. Drive your body weight and crossing (right) knee as far to the left as possible. Jumping up is a waste of energy and time. Strive for distance, not height.
5. After thrusting, the left leg (now the free leg) must immediately return, pass the contact (right) foot in the V (heel to heel) posi-

a

b

c

d

e

f

g

Figure 8.7   Side (crossover) start sequence.

tion, and reach forward in preparation for becoming the new contact foot (Figure 8.7f).

The Second Stride

As the right foot contacts the ice it becomes the new pushing foot.

1. One crossover is sufficient. As you push with your right leg, pivot your hips to face forward. The next and all subsequent strides will be the powerful sprinting steps of the front start.
2. When your left foot takes the ice as the new contact foot it should land on the front 2 to 3 inches of the inside edge, your body weight centered over the edge, heel unweighted (Figure 8.7g), just as in the second step of the front start.
3. After thrusting, the right leg (now the free leg) must immediately return, pass the left foot in the V position, and reach forward to become the new contact foot.

Subsequent Strides

On the third or fourth stride the skates will begin to glide, and the angle of your upper body to the ice should gradually become more upright until, after six or seven strides, it is in the forward stride position (approximately 45 degrees to the ice).

POINTS TO REMEMBER

- On the crossover your contact skate must touch down sideways (approximately 70 degrees) to the line of travel or the edge won't dig in properly. Figure 8.8 diagrams the cuts made in the ice when the side start sequence is correctly performed.
- Use the outside leg push during the crossover to shift your body weight to the side. Use the inside leg push to drive outward and onto the new contact foot.
- Use the blade edges to grip the ice. Drive the pushing leg directly against the grip. Do not let the pushing skate slip back.
- Keep your head up and shoulders level for balance and stability.

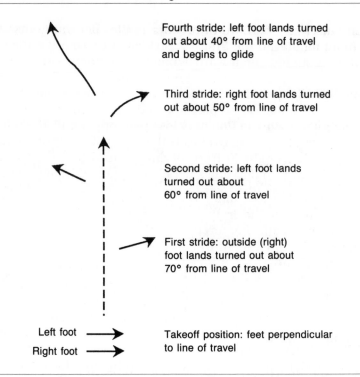

Fourth stride: left foot lands turned out about 40° from line of travel and begins to glide

Third stride: right foot lands turned out about 50° from line of travel

Second stride: left foot lands turned out about 60° from line of travel

First stride: outside (right) foot lands turned out about 70° from line of travel

Left foot ⟶
Right foot ⟶

Takeoff position: feet perpendicular to line of travel

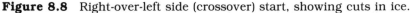

Figure 8.8   Right-over-left side (crossover) start, showing cuts in ice.

Backward Starts

It is important to achieve explosive backward acceleration from a stationary position so that you won't have to turn your back on the play. Hockey players who have not mastered the backward start are at the disadvantage of having to start forward and then wheel around backward to face the play. A defender must be able to start backward quickly to remain ahead of and facing the onrushing opposition.

When starting backward you cannot angle your upper body as you can with the front or side starts or you will fall over backward. Therefore, you are limited in how much you can drive your weight in the direction of travel (backward). Because of this limitation the backward start does not generate speed as rapidly as forward or side starts.

There are two methods of starting out backward. One is the

straight backward start, and the other is the backward crossover start. As in all starts, the first few strides of these are critical.

All players should aim toward achieving confidence in these two starts. In a game you may sometimes find one more advantageous than the other, depending on the situation. For example, it is important that as a defending player you do not commit yourself to one direction too soon, or you may lose your opponent. The advantage of the straight backward start is that you will skate on a course that keeps you straight in front of and neutral to the opponent, rather than committed to one side. If the opponent makes a move to one side you can cross over or turn to that side and cut him or her off. But because it is a slower start, you risk getting passed while you're accelerating. If the opponent is pressing, you may be better off using the backward crossover start.

The backward crossover start has the disadvantage of committing the player to one side. This can open a hole for the opponent to break through. Forwards always look for the defender to cross over prematurely and use this mistake to break through. So when using the crossover start there should be some room between you and the opposition or you stand a good chance of "getting burned."

NOTE: In situations where the opposing forward is closely pressing the defender, the defender may have to start forward, build speed, and then turn backward. But whenever possible, start backward so you are facing the play.

The Straight Backward Start

This start is used primarily in situations where the defender wants to stay neutral to the opponent.

To perform the straight backward start execute a sequence of backward C-cut pushes. The gliding foot must aim straight backward. The difference between the straight backward start and the straight backward stride is that the legs move much more rapidly on the initial steps. The contact foot should glide as little as possible, but each pushing leg must thrust and return through its full range of motion. See chapter 7 for details on the C-cut push procedure.

NOTE: Although the start requires a very rapid leg rhythm, be sure to get full leg drive and full leg recovery.

1. The inside edge is employed as the thrusting edge, as it is in the C-cut pushes of straight backward skating. Bend your

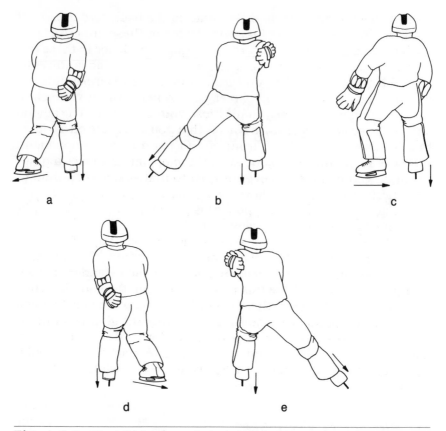

Figure 8.9   Straight backward start sequence.

knees deeply, pivot the heel of the thrusting skate outward, all
your weight over the pushing leg, and dig the inside edge into
the ice to prepare for pushing (Figure 8.9a).

2. Cut the C by thrusting against the inside edge. Use the front
   half of the blade length to push against the ice. The final thrust
   is made with the toe of the inside edge. Push powerfully and
   explosively for optimum thrust (Figure 8.9b).
3. The C-cut push must be executed to full extension. The pushing leg must then recover rapidly so the other leg can push
   immediately (Figures 8.9c, d, and e).
4. After several pushes you should approach top speed.
5. Swing your arms along the same line of force and in rhythm
   with your legs. As your right leg thrusts forward and outward,
   your right arm goes back, and vice versa.

POINTS TO REMEMBER

- Speed is the result of powerful leg drive and rapid leg motion. Small, hopping steps provide little thrust and take you nowhere.
- Keep your hips and shoulders facing directly backward. If they turn sideways with each push you will waddle side to side rather than skate straight backward.
- Keep the contact (gliding) foot pointing straight backward.
- When making the C-cut, be sure the entire blade length is in contact with the ice surface. If you lift your heel off the ice your weight will rock forward over the toe and you will be off balance.
- Keep your shoulders held back, back upright, and head up to avoid pitching over the curved toes.

Backward Crossover Start

The backward crossover start is the method generally preferred to accelerate backward. Many players feel they generate speed faster with this start than with the straight backward start.

Like the straight backward start, the backward crossover start begins with the powerful C-cut thrust. To perform the backward crossover start execute the C-cut thrust to full extension before crossing over (Figures 8.10a and b). Then cross the inside leg under your body in a scissor thrust as the other leg (now the free leg) crosses over (Figures 8.10c and d). (See chapter 7, "Weaving Crossovers," for details of the procedure.) As in all starts, drive your legs powerfully and rapidly. Figure 8.11 diagrams the backward crossover start.

Exercises for Improving Starts

These exercises are designed specifically for improving forward, side, and backward starts.

Figure 8.10 Backward crossover start sequence.

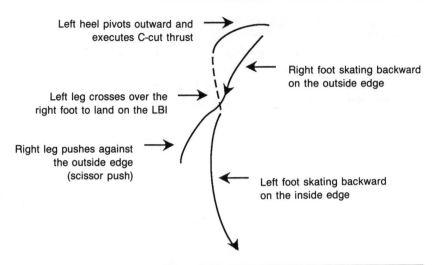

Left heel pivots outward and executes C-cut thrust

Right foot skating backward on the outside edge

Left leg crosses over the right foot to land on the LBI

Right leg pushes against the outside edge (scissor push)

Left foot skating backward on the inside edge

Figure 8.11   Pattern of backward crossover start: Try to travel as straight backward as possible.

Forward (Front) Start Exercises

The following exercises will help you develop the coordination, edge control, and body angulation necessary for explosive forward starts.

The Penguin

To do this exercise you walk across the ice on the "toes" in a penguinlike manner.

1. Place your feet in an exaggerated V position, heels together, toes apart, feet turned outward about 80 degrees from the line of travel.
2. Bend your knees deeply. Your knees and toes should be well turned out.
3. Keeping your knees bent, roll in your ankles until the lower leg and the inside edge of each skate form an angle of 45 degrees with the ice. Keep your heels together, toes apart.
4. Place your weight over the front 2 to 3 inches of the inside edges and lift your heels so that only the fronts of the edges are in contact with the ice. Maintain the same edge angle and knee bend while standing in this position (Figure 8.12a).
5. Walk across the ice in this manner, always touching down on the front 2 to 3 inches of the inside edge (45-degree angle), with heels elevated, knees bent, knees and feet turned out, and body

weight pressing downward over the engaged edge (Figure 8.12b).

6. To walk in this position your heels must be pointed in and toes pointed out as each foot passes the other.

7. Do not allow the contact skate to glide. The marks in the ice should be 2 to 3 inches long, indicating no glide.

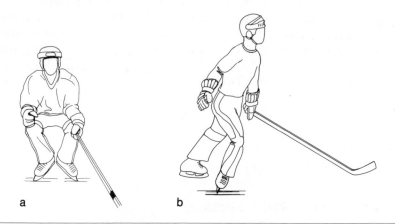

a   b

Figure 8.12   The penguin exercise.

Running on the Toes

Run in place on the inside edges of the blades, always maintaining the exaggerated penguin-like V position—heels pointed in, knees and toes pointed out. Keep your heels off the ice and your weight on the front 2 to 3 inches of the inside edges as you run.

Variation:

Do the same exercise, but instead of running in place, run between the blue lines. Push to full extension. Do not allow the contact skate to glide!

Starts Against the Boards

This exercise trains you to reach the knee of the contact foot forward for distance rather than upward for height. It also develops the feeling of angling the body forward, of fully extending the pushing leg while reaching the front knee forward, and of maintaining the turned-out (V) position of the feet through the push and return.

1. Stand facing the boards at arm's length from them. Hold on to them with both hands.
2. Turn your feet in the exaggerated V position, heels turned in, knees and toes turned out.
3. Angle your body forward but keep your back straight.
4. Run in place, reaching your front knee forward on each step to touch the boards in the turned out position. The contact skate should take the ice in the V position (heel in, toe out) with your weight on the front 2 to 3 inches of the inside edge, heel off the ice. Keep your heels in and toes out as each foot passes the other.
5. As you reach the front knee forward to the boards, drive your pushing (back) leg to full extension (Figure 8.13).

Figure 8.13   Forward starts at the boards.

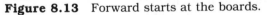

Resistance

The purpose of this exercise is to reach the knee of the contact foot forward for distance while driving the pushing leg to full extension and taking each running stride on the toe of the inside edge.

Push another player down the ice while running on the inside blade edges of your toes. The player going backward should resist by doing a two-foot backward snowplow stop (see chapter 9). Keep your heels off the ice as you run (Figures 8.14a and b). Note the strong forward angle of the upper body of the pushing player in Figure 8.14b.

a   b

Figure 8.14   Resistance exercise on toes.

Forward Starts Over Hockey Sticks

Forward starts over hockey sticks train your legs to drive harder and your upper body to shift out farther in order to achieve more distance on the front start. Concentrate on driving yourself outward for distance, not upward for height.

Team up with three other players of similar height and ability. Place four sticks on the ice, as diagrammed in Figure 8.15. The sticks should be spaced so that the upper body must shift well forward and each driving stride must cover more distance than the one before it. Distances must vary with the skater's size and ability. Make the distances challenging but not impossible to achieve. If the sticks are placed too close together you will jump upward to get over them rather than outward to get past them. This would be counterproductive.

1. Face the sticks and stand with your toes almost touching the first stick.
2. Pivot your feet into the exaggerated V position.
3. Place your weight over the thrusting (right) foot, bend both knees, and dig the inside edge of your thrusting skate into the

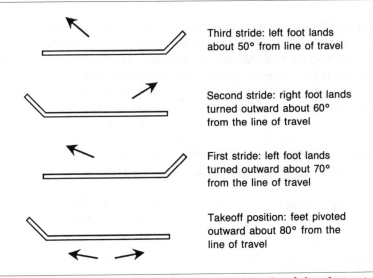

Third stride: left foot lands about 50° from line of travel

Second stride: right foot lands turned outward about 60° from the line of travel

First stride: left foot lands turned outward about 70° from the line of travel

Takeoff position: feet pivoted outward about 80° from the line of travel

Figure 8.15   Forward start over sticks; note angle of the skates to the line of travel.

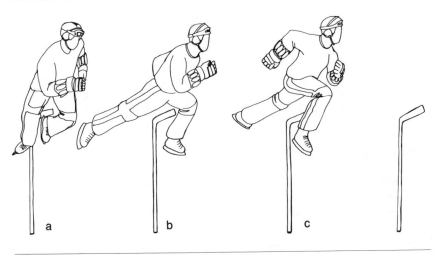

Figure 8.16   Forward start over sticks.

ice (45 degrees). Project your body weight low and well forward (see Figure 8.16a).

4. Leap beyond the first two sticks, landing past the second stick on the front 2 to 3 inches of the left inside edge. Make certain your left skate lands turned out in the V position, body weight over it, heel off the ice (Figure 8.16b). As in all front starts, the cut should be short and turned-out. Do not glide.

5. Repeat the procedure, thrusting with your left leg and landing beyond the third stick on the front 2 to 3 inches of the right

skate's inside edge, body weight over it, with your skate turned out (Figure 8.16c). Do not glide.

6. Thrust again with your right leg, landing past the fourth stick on your left skate's inside edge with your left foot turned out. After you have passed the fourth stick, keep sprinting until you reach top speed. Your body angle should rise gradually until, when you reach top speed, it is at a 45-degree angle to the ice.

7. As the exercise becomes easier, separate the sticks further. Force the legs to drive hard to clear the sticks, but don't make it impossible. Remember: Don't leap up to pass the sticks, leap out!

8. Repeat, using your left skate and leg to make the initial thrust. The legs must be equally capable of making the all-important first thrust.

Take the sticks away and see if you can go as far or farther than you did with the sticks. Move your legs as rapidly as possible. Do not slow your leg speed in trying to go farther.

Sprint Starts

Start from the goal line. Take two or three running strides and then sprint to the first blue line. Time yourself. Remember: Combine quickness, power, and distance on the starting strides and try to improve your time.

Side (Crossover) Start Exercises

The following exercises help develop the coordination, edge control, and body weight projection necessary for explosive side starts. Practice them using both the left and right legs to perform the initial thrust.

Walking Crossovers

Stand facing perpendicular to your intended direction of travel. Walk to the left, crossing your right foot over your left foot as you walk sideways. The left (leading or inside) skate should always step onto its outside edge, then cross under the body to push. The right (trailing or outside) skate should, after pushing, cross over the left foot and step onto its inside edge. Start on one side of the rink and walk all the way across. Keep your feet at right angles to your line of travel at all times.

Leaping Crossovers

Follow the above procedure, but leap sideways along your line of travel on the front 2 to 3 inches of the edges. Keep your heels off the ice and leap outward, not upward.

Variations:

1. Repeat the above exercise, trying to get as much sideways distance as possible from each stride. Use the push from your outside leg to shift your weight out to the side. Use the push from your inside leg to move you out to the side. Keep the heel of your contact skate off the ice.
2. Skate forward along the boards, starting from the goal line (Figure 8.17). Stop at the near blue line. Do lateral leaping crossovers (left over right) along the blue line across to the opposite sideboards. Stop. Skate forward to the far blue line, stop, and do lateral leaping crossovers (right over left) along the blue line to the opposite sideboards. Stop, skate forward along the boards to the goal line, and stop again.

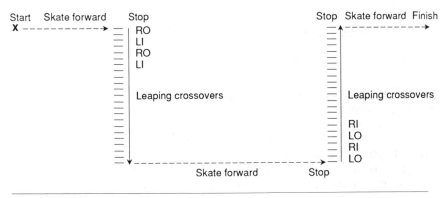

Figure 8.17   Leaping crossovers.

Whistle Drill

On a whistle signal rapidly move sideways to the left, using leaping crossovers (right over left). Get as much sideways distance and move your legs as quickly as possible. On a second signal, stop and drive the other way (to the right), left over right. Keep alternating directions on the whistle signals. Keep your heels off the ice and your feet and body at right angles to the line of travel.

Side (Crossover) Starts Over Hockey Sticks

Crossover starts over hockey sticks train the legs to drive harder and the upper body to shift out farther to the side in order to achieve more distance on crossover starts. Concentrate on driving yourself outward for distance, not upward for height.

Team up with three other players of similar height and ability. Place four sticks on the ice, as diagrammed in Figure 8.18.

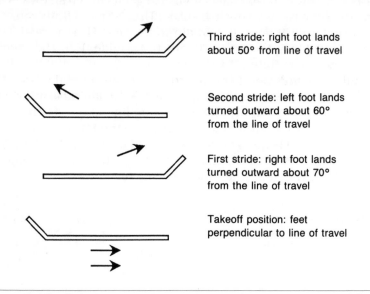

Third stride: right foot lands about 50° from line of travel

Second stride: left foot lands turned outward about 60° from the line of travel

First stride: right foot lands turned outward about 70° from the line of travel

Takeoff position: feet perpendicular to line of travel

Figure 8.18   Side (crossover) start over sticks; note position of feet to the line of travel.

1. Stand facing parallel to the sticks (perpendicular to your direction of travel) with the sticks to your left. Place your left foot as close to the first stick as possible, with your right foot parallel to your left, feet about shoulder width apart, knees bent, with weight over your outside skate.
2. Do a crossover start. Thrust your right leg to full extension, using it to shift your weight to the left (Figure 8.19a).
3. Drive your left leg under your body, and at the same time do a leaping crossover, crossing your right foot over your left and landing on the right skate beyond the second stick. Land on the front 2 to 3 inches of the inside edge of your right skate, with your right skate still sideways (about 70 degrees) to the line of travel (Figure 8.19b). Keep the heel off the ice and do

not glide when you touch down. If your heel touches the ice you will glide.

4. Pivot your hips, chest, and shoulders 90 degrees until you face fully forward in the front start position, then immediately thrust your right leg against the right inside edge as you would in a front start. Leap forward to land past the third stick on the front 2 to 3 inches of the inside edge of your left skate, your weight over it and your heel off the ice. Your left foot should touch down in a well-turned-out position as in the front start, so the inside edge can instantly grip the ice (Figure 8.19c).

5. Thrust again with your left leg and leap forward as in the front start. Leap beyond the fourth stick, landing on the right inside edge with the right foot turned outward. Continue sprinting until you reach full speed. Your body angle should rise gradually until it reaches the skating angle of the forward stride (approximately 45 degrees).

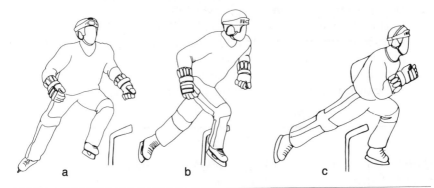

a   b   c

Figure 8.19   Side (crossover) start over sticks.

To execute the exercise in the opposite direction, face the other way. Your right foot will now be close to the first stick and you will leap to the right, crossing left over right.

The sticks should be spaced so that the legs are forced to push powerfully, the upper body is forced to shift outward, and so that each stride takes you further than the previous one. As in forward starts, distances between the sticks must be challenging and adjusted to fit the height and ability of each player. Although the sticks force you to jump up a bit to clear them, concentrate on leaping beyond them (farther) rather than over them (higher). Then take the sticks away and see if you can get more distance on your crossover start in the same or less time as before. Measure how far outward you travel on the first three strides of the start (one crossover, two forward steps) in as short a time as possible. Keep trying to increase the distance and shorten the time. Remember: More distance covered in the same or less time means a faster start!

Side Starts Over the Goal Crease

This exercise is similar to leaping over sticks in that the outer line of the goal crease acts as a target for the legs. The purpose is to train the legs to push and the body weight to shift to the side more effectively. More weight projection into the side start helps achieve greater distance on the starting strides.

1. Stand facing parallel to the goal line (perpendicular to your line of travel). Place your left (leading or inside) foot on the goal line and your right foot parallel to your left, feet about shoulder width apart, knees bent, weight over your outside foot.
2. Do a leaping crossover (right over left) and try to land as close to the outer crease line as possible. Land on the front 2 to 3 inches of the right inside edge, your right foot parallel to the line of the crease, 70 degrees from the line of travel. Then pivot forward and sprint to the blue line.
3. Repeat, doing a left-over-right crossover start.

Sprint Starts

Start from the goal line. Using the side (crossover) start, take two or three running steps and then sprint to the first blue line. Alternate the side to which you start and try to better your time both ways.

Backward Start Exercises

The following exercises help develop explosive backward starts.

Straight Backward Start

1. Stand close to and face the boards. Place your weight over your left (pushing) leg, bend your left knee deeply, and dig the left inside edge into the ice. Aim your right (gliding) skate straight back. Cut a C-cut push with the left inside edge, using strong leg drive to execute the thrust. Bring the thrusting foot back

under your body as rapidly as possible after completing the thrust. Then execute a backward C-cut thrust with the right leg. Cut a total of three C-cut thrusts, moving your legs as rapidly as possible. Be sure to travel straight back. Come to a stop after the third C-cut and check to see how far you have traveled after three pushes. Repeat, trying to increase the distance and shorten the time. Do the same exercise with your right leg performing the initial push.

2. Perform the exercise pulling a player who creates a resistance by doing a forward snowplow stop as you do the backward start. The resisting player should hold one end of a hockey stick as you hold the other end. Keep the stick chest high and horizontal. Refer to the "Resistance" exercise, chapter 6 ("The Straight Backward Stride") for the procedure.

3. Starting from the goal line, time yourself to the first blue line as you do backward C-cut thrusts. Try to reduce your time. Be sure to alternate the starting leg so that each leg develops the power and coordination to act as the initial thrusting leg.

Backward Crossover Start

1. Perform step 1 of the Straight Backward Start just described, but now execute the exercise as a series of backward crossovers.

2. Perform step 2 of the previous exercise (pulling a resisting player), now doing backward crossover starts.

3. Doing backward crossover starts, time yourself from the goal line to the first blue line. Remember to alternate the leg that executes the initial push.

4. Practice starts with another skater, one acting as forward, the other as defender. See Figure 6.7, chapter 6, for a description of this exercise.

Chapter

9

STOPS

Learning to stop is essential to playing effective hockey. Mastering a variety of stops enables you to change directions instantly as the puck changes hands, or to stop gradually if the situation requires. Sudden stops are as vital as quick starts.

Forward Stops

The forward stops covered in this section progress from the most elementary to the most difficult.

Two-Foot Snowplow Stop

The two-foot snowplow stop—like the skier's snowplow—is the easiest stop to learn and therefore the first stop taught to beginners. In game situations it is used only for slowing down or stopping gradually. It is inadequate for very sudden stops.

1. Glide straight ahead on two skates, feet shoulder width apart.
2. Turn both heels outward so that your toes point toward each other in an inverted V position (pigeon-toed position). Keep your body facing the line of travel.
3. Using *slight* inside edges on both skates, scrape against the ice. As you scrape against the ice, force your heels still farther

Figure 9.1 Two-foot snowplow stop.

apart, and bend your knees (Figure 9.1). Try to bring up "snow" with your blade edges.

POINTS TO REMEMBER

- Keep your weight on the balls of your feet. If you try to scrape with your heels, the edges may catch the ice and stopping will be difficult.
- Keep your shoulders back, back straight, and head up. If you lean forward, you will pitch over your toes.
- Use slight inside edges to stop. If you edge too deeply, they will dig into the ice and you will have trouble stopping.
- Imagine that you want to scrape the ice to bring up snow; don't try to cut into it.
- Keep the entire blade lengths of both skates in contact with the ice. Lifting the heels will cause you to pitch over your toes.

One-Foot Snowplow Stop

The one-foot snowplow stop is sometimes used in game situations. Defenders may use it, for instance, when they are skating forward but want to decelerate to prepare for skating backward, or if they want to stop gradually. Goaltenders frequently use the one-foot snowplow stop.

1. Glide straight ahead on the flat of the left skate, keeping it centered under your body.
2. Holding your right foot somewhat out in front, turn the toe inward (pigeon-toed) and press your right skate against the ice, using a slight inside edge to scrape against the ice.
3. Bend your right knee to press your weight downward over your right skate as it scrapes against the ice in the pigeon-toed position (Figure 9.2).
4. Apply pressure to the ice with the ball of the foot.
5. Except for pigeon-toeing and scraping against the ice with only one foot rather than both, the stop is performed in the same way as the two-foot snowplow.
6. Repeat, using the left foot to pigeon-toe and execute the stop, with the right foot now gliding straight ahead.

Figure 9.2   One-foot snowplow stop.

T Stop

The T stop is used often when you are coming to the bench or the face-off circle but rarely in instances when sudden, well-balanced stops are demanded.

1. Glide forward on the flat of your right skate.

2. Pick up your left foot and place it behind your right foot, turning the toe outward so that the foot is perpendicular to the front foot. Your feet should form an inverted T.
3. Place the outside edge of your back (left) foot on the ice (in this perpendicular position), and bend the left knee. Apply gradual pressure to the ice by scraping with the outside edge. Use the ball of your foot to scrape the ice (Figure 9.3a).
4. Keep your shoulders level as you lean back to stop. If you lower your back shoulder, you will fall backward.
5. Stop by scraping the ice with the outside edge. If you lean forward you will be forced to drag the inside edge (Figure 9.3b) and won't be able to stop quickly or efficiently.

a   b

c

Figure 9.3   T stop: (a) correct position; (b) incorrect; (c) on one foot.

6. Your shoulders, chest, and hips should face forward when executing this stop.
7. Advanced skaters often do a T stop completely on the back foot; the front foot is actually off the ice (Figure 9.3c).

Be sure to master both the one-foot snowplow and the T stop, since together they make up the hockey stop.

Hockey Stop

Hockey often demands that you stop suddenly to stay with the play or to change directions as the action shifts. The hockey stop is the most efficient of all stops and is therefore the stop used in most game situations. It is effective not only because it allows a player to stop suddenly but also because it is a very stable and well-balanced stop. Players must be able to stop instantly and with confidence both to the right and left sides so they can always stop facing the action.

The hockey stop involves turning sideways to the line of travel.

1. Skate straight forward. Glide very briefly in preparation for stopping. Then turn your shoulders, chest, hips, knees, and feet sharply to the left (Figure 9.4a). If this maneuver were done on a straight line, it would be a 90-degree change of direction (Figure 9.4b).
2. To stop, first unbend your knees slightly, to release your weight; do this as you turn sideways. Then bend your knees deeply and reapply your weight firmly downward toward the ice. This downward pressure combined with the sideways turn causes the edges to scrape the ice, bringing you to a stop. The greater the knee bend and downward pressure, the quicker you will stop.
3. The hockey stop is generally executed with the body weight distributed approximately 60% on the front (outside) foot and 40% on the back (inside) foot. This guideline varies according to game demands.
4. Your front (outside) foot scrapes the ice with its inside edge, while your back (inside) foot scrapes the ice with its outside edge. Try to scrape up snow as you stop. The faster you are going and the more suddenly you press your weight down toward the ice as you stop, the more snow you will scrape up.
5. Scrape the ice with the balls of your feet. Scraping with your heels causes the edges to dig into the ice too much and you will have trouble stopping smoothly.
6. To stop to the right, mirror the above procedures.
7. During the stop the upper body usually turns sideways along

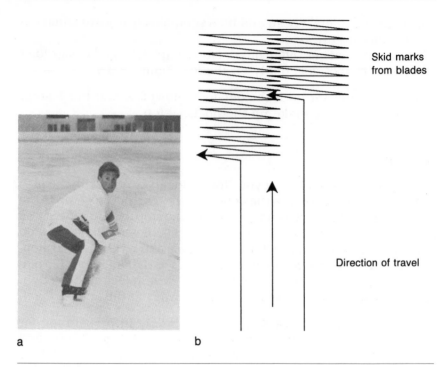

Skid marks
from blades

Direction of travel

a   b

Figure 9.4   Hockey stop to the left.

with the hips, knees, and feet, which puts you in an excellent position to use a crossover start to skate either forward in the same direction or back the opposite way.

When you need to stop and then skate backward in the direction from which you just came, this variation of the hockey stop can

Figure 9.5   Hockey stop: upper body faces forward.

be used: As you execute the stop, keep your chest and shoulders facing forward. Do not turn them fully sideways as you turn your hips, knees, and feet (Figure 9.5). This way your upper body remains in position to move backward. This is advantageous for starting backward quickly in game situations.

POINTS TO REMEMBER

- Keep your feet shoulder width or even slightly wider apart during the stop. If your feet are too close together your balance will be precarious. You will also be in a poor position to shift your weight into a start.
- Hold your shoulders back and level to the ice and keep your head up. Your back (trailing) shoulder corresponds to the inside shoulder on a curve; lowering it may cause you to lose your balance and fall.
- Keep the entire blade lengths of both skates on the ice when you stop.
- Glide briefly before turning sideways to stop.

One-Foot Stops

One-foot stops are similar in execution to the hockey stop, except that the body weight is concentrated on only one foot. There are two variations—the front-foot stop and the back-foot stop.

1. *Front-foot*: Skate forward, gliding on your right foot, and pick up the left foot. Turn your body 90 degrees to the left, bend your right knee, and scrape the ice with the inside edge of your right (front) foot until you stop. Keep your left (back) foot off the ice during the stop (Figure 9.6). Repeat on the left foot, turning your body and stopping to the right.
2. *Back-foot*: Skate forward, gliding on your right foot, left foot off the ice. Turn your body 90 degrees to the right, bend your right knee and scrape the ice with the outside edge of your right (back) skate. Keep your left (front) foot off the ice during the stop (Figure 9.3c). When using the left foot as the back foot, turn sideways to the left.

Figure 9.6   Front-foot stop.

You must lean much farther back than in the front-foot or hockey stops to stop with the outside edge of the back foot, but otherwise the stop is executed similarly. If you lower your back (trailing) shoulder, your foot may slip out from under you.

Backward Stops

Backward stops are imperative for playing defense or skating backward.

Two-Foot Backward Snowplow Stop

This stop is used to stop quickly and efficiently when skating backward.

1. Glide straight backward on two skates, keeping them about shoulder width apart. Rotate the toes of both feet outward while rotating the heels inward. Your feet should approximate a V position. You cannot stop with your feet parallel to each other.
2. Push the toes of both feet farther apart. As you do this, your heels will also separate to about shoulder width apart.
3. As your toes rotate outward, press against the ice with *slight* inside edges of both skates and scrape the ice with the edges.
4. Bend your knees deeply as the edges scrape the ice. The more

your knees bend, the more pressure you will exert downward against the ice and the quicker you'll stop.

5. Scrape the ice equally with both skates by keeping your weight equally distributed. Use the balls of your feet to scrape the ice (Figure 9.7).

Figure 9.7   Two-foot backward snowplow stop.

A well-executed backward snowplow stop leaves the player in a good position to start forward. To thrust off forward, shift your weight onto the leg that is to push, dig the inside edge of the thrusting skate into the ice, bend the knee more deeply, and push off (Figure 9.8). It is important that when stopping the heels are about shoulder width apart. If your heels separate farther than shoulder width during the stop, there is a delay in getting the thrusting leg re-centered under the body for a forward thrust.

Figure 9.8   Stop backward, start forward.

POINTS TO REMEMBER

- Lean slightly forward, away from the stop, but keep your back straight and your head up.
- Keep hips, chest, and shoulders facing straight ahead.

One-Foot Backward Snowplow Stop

The one-foot backward snowplow stop is similar to the two-foot backward snowplow stop, except that only one foot executes the stop.

1. Glide straight backward on the flats of both skates.
2. To stop with your right foot, shift your weight over your right foot and rotate the toe of your right skate outward (the heel rotates inward).
3. Bending your right knee deeply, scrape the ice with the inside edge of the right skate, using a slight to moderate edge. Scrape the ice with the ball of the foot (Figure 9.9).

Figure 9.9 One-foot backward stop.

This stop leaves you in excellent position for a quick forward start, because the stopping foot is directly under your body weight and turned outward in the front start position. All you have to do is dig the inside edge deeper into the ice, bend your knee more deeply, and thrust off forward (Figure 9.8).

Exercises for Improving Stops

The following exercises are designed to develop the coordination, edge control, and body weight distribution needed to execute effective stops.

Snowplow Stops

1. Stand in place and scrape the ice simultaneously with both skates by pressing the feet apart in a pigeon-toed position. Try to make "snow" by using the balls of the feet and slight inside edges to scrape the ice.
2. Swizzles: These develop the turn-out/turn-in coordination necessary for snowplow stops. Swizzles are explained in chapter 3.
3. Start at the boards and skate forward across the ice, stopping at the other side with a two-foot snowplow stop. Do not touch the boards. Hold the hockey stick chest-high, horizontally, arms extended, to avoid leaning on it when stopping.
4. Repeat, using the one-foot snowplow stop. Alternate between left and right feet as the snowplowing skate.
5. Start from the goal line and skate forward, stopping and then starting again as you reach the first blue line, the center red line, the second blue line, and the far goal line. Use one-foot snowplow stops at each line, alternating left and right feet.

Backward snowplow drills are executed exactly the same way; only the direction is reversed.

Team-Up Hockey Stop

For those just learning the hockey stop it may be useful to work with an instructor, or partner. This allows you to concentrate on learning to coordinate the feet, knees, and hips without having to worry about controlling your upper body, which will be controlled by the instructor or partner via the stick.

1. Face the instructor (or partner), holding a hockey stick horizontally and chest high between you. The instructor should skate backward. You (the student) should now glide forward on two skates.
2. On the instructor's signal, turn your hips and feet 90 degrees to the right and bend your knees. Keeping your feet parallel to each other, scrape the ice with the inside edge of the front foot and the outside edge of the back foot and try to stop (Figure 9.10).

Repeat, turning your hips, knees, and feet to the left. Be sure to work on the direction that is more difficult.

Figure 9.10   Team-up hockey stop.

Hockey Stops on the Whistle

1. Stand at the goal line, prepared to skate forward.
2. On a whistle signal, skate forward.
3. On the next whistle, briefly glide, then do a hockey stop, facing the sideboards to your left. Be sure to come to a complete stop.
4. On the next whistle, skate forward again in the same direction.
5. On the next whistle, stop again, facing the same way.

Do this the entire length of the ice. Coming back, stop facing the same sideboards (now to your right). This way you will work on hockey stops to both sides.

Exercises for Improving Stops and Starts

When hockey players come to sudden stops, they do so knowing they will probably have to immediately start out again suddenly and explosively. Stops, in fact, set up the upcoming starts, so the quality of the stop affects the quality of the start which follows. For example: Stopping with your feet too close together limits your ability to shift your weight in the desired direction to start, thereby limiting the distance you can achieve on the first stride. Stopping on unbent knees leaves you uncoiled for the next start, putting you flatfooted and out of the play. Since stops and starts are so interrelated they should be practiced together as well as separately. The following exercises are designed with that in mind.

When doing exercises for stops and starts it is important to work on improving the weaker side. On every exercise be sure to stop to both sides and to alternate the initial thrusting leg of the start. Do this by skating up and down one side of the rink and stopping so that you always face the same sideboards. While skating one way you will always stop facing your left and then use left-over-right crossovers to restart, and while going the other way you will stop facing right and use right-over-left crossover starts. If stopping or starting in a particular direction is weaker, give it extra attention.

Hockey Stops/Forward and Crossover Starts

Exercise 1

1. Do a forward (front) start from the goal line and sprint forward to the first blue line. Do a hockey stop, turning to the left (Figure 9.11a).
2. Start out again with a left-over-right crossover start (Figures 9.11b and c). Do one crossover then pivot forward and sprint forward to the center red line. Stop as before.
3. Do another crossover start and sprint forward to the second blue line. Stop as before.
4. Do a crossover start and sprint forward to the far goal line. Stop as before.
5. Repeat the exercise, skating back down the ice, stopping and starting to the other side.

Variation:

Repeat the exercise but instead of stopping and starting at the lines, stop and start on whistle signals.

Figure 9.11   Exercise 1: Stop and start, continuing in same direction.

Exercise 2

In this exercise all stops and starts must face the same sideboards.

1. Start at the goal line with a forward start and sprint forward to the first blue line. Do a hockey stop to the left (Figure 9.12a).
2. Reverse directions with a right-over-left crossover start (Figures 9.12b and c) and sprint forward to the original goal line. Stop there, turning to the right to face the same sideboards.
3. Reverse directions again with a left-over-right crossover start. This time sprint forward to the center red line. Stop to the left.
4. Repeat step 2 (return to goal line).

Figure 9.12   Exercise 2: Stop and start, continuing in opposite direction.

5. Reverse directions with a left-over-right crossover start, and sprint forward to the far blue line. Stop to the left.
6. Repeat step 2 again (return to goal line).
7. Reverse once more, using a left-over-right crossover start. Sprint forward to the far goal line and stop to the left.
8. Repeat step 2 (return to original goal line).
9. Repeat the exercise, stopping and starting to the other sides.

Variation:

Repeat the exercise, but instead of stopping and starting at the lines, stop and start on whistle signals.

Exercise 3

Do a hockey stop to your left, with your body weight primarily on your front (outside) foot.

1. To continue in the same direction: After stopping, shift your weight to the right, from over the right inside edge to over the right outside edge. Now you are ready for a left-over-right crossover start.
2. To skate back in the opposite direction: Keep your weight on the right inside edge. You now have two options:
   - Pivot your hips to face forward and do a front start.
   - Do a right-over-left crossover start. To do this, push with your right leg and shift your weight far to the left until it is over the left outside edge and then drive into the crossover start.

Stops are usually performed with about 60% of the body weight over the front (outside) foot. However, there are exceptions to this, as shown in the following exercise.

Exercise 4

Perform a hockey stop to the left, with your weight primarily over your back (inside) foot.

1. To continue in the same direction you can do either a front start or a side start.
   - To use the front start, shift your weight from the left outside edge onto the left inside edge, pivot your hips to face fully forward, and do the front start.

- To use the side start, first shift your weight from the left outside edge onto the left inside edge. Continue shifting your weight to the right until it is over the right foot, outside edge, and then thrust into a left-over-right crossover start (Figures 9.11a, b, and c).

2. To skate back in the opposite direction:

- Use a right-over-left crossover start. Just shift your weight farther out over the left outside edge and thrust into the side start (Figures 9.12a, b, and c).
- A front start in the opposite direction is possible, but the back-foot stop leaves you well prepared for an explosive crossover start. The front start entails first pivoting your body to face forward and therefore may not be as quick or explosive.

Forward Stops/Backward Starts

When you anticipate having to stop and then go backward, use a forward stop that will prepare you to start backward quickly. For example, use either the one-foot snowplow stop or a hockey stop with your weight primarily over the front (outside) foot. It may be advantageous to use the hockey stop variation in which your upper body does not turn fully sideways as you stop (see Figure 9.5). If using the one-foot snowplow stop, the stopping foot of the snowplow, which corresponds to the front foot of the hockey stop, becomes the thrusting leg for the backward start. Similarly, the front foot of the hockey stop becomes the thrusting leg of the backward start. Remember: The initial thrust of the backward start is the C-cut thrust.

Because the front leg of the forward stop is to become the thrusting leg of the backward start, it is critical to keep your weight primarily on your front leg while stopping. Your body weight is then correctly positioned over the pushing leg for the backward C-cut thrust (Figure 9.13a). Too many players stop with their weight almost completely over their back leg and therefore cannot push effectively into the backward start. When doing a backward crossover start, be sure to use the crossunder push immediately following the C-cut thrust (Figures 9.13b, c, and d).

NOTE: When you start out backward from any hockey stop position, you must turn your hips 90 degrees or one quarter turn as you start so they will be square to your new line of travel. Turn them as you execute the C-cut thrust, not before the C-cut, or it will delay your start. Don't turn them farther than 1/4 turn or your new line of travel will be altered, forcing you to skate side to side rather than straight backward.

d

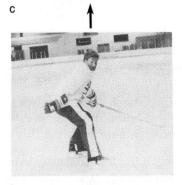

c

b

a

Figure 9.13   Start backward, using backward crossover start.

Exercise 1

Use this exercise to improve forward stops followed by straight backward starts.

1. Glide forward on your right foot with your left foot off the ice. Stop (turning to the left) on your right foot. This is a front-foot hockey stop.
2. Keeping your left foot off the ice, roll your right skate onto its inside edge and bend the right knee so the edge and the lower leg form an approximately 45-degree angle to the ice. Execute a backward C-cut, pushing with your right leg.
3. During the push, shift your weight onto the flat of your left skate and glide straight backward on the left skate.
4. Stop. Mirror the procedure and repeat the drill, stopping on and executing the backward C-cut push with your left leg.

Exercise 2

Perform this exercise to improve forward stops followed by backward crossover starts.

1. Perform Exercise 1. However, as you execute the backward C-cut thrust with your right leg, shift your weight onto and skate backward on the outside edge of your left skate rather than the flat of the blade.
2. Push with the left outside edge, crossing the leg under your body. Your right foot should cross over and take the ice gliding backward on its inside edge as the pushing leg crosses under.
3. Stop. Mirror the procedure, executing the C-cut thrust with your left leg and the crossunder push with your right leg.

Exercise 3

1. Do a front start from one sideboards and sprint forward across the ice. Execute the initial push of the start with your right leg.
2. Stop at the opposite sideboards using a hockey stop to the left, and prepare to skate backward.
3. Do a right-over-left backward crossover start and sprint backward to your original position.
4. Stop at the original sideboards using a one-foot backward snowplow stop with your right foot, and prepare to skate forward again.

5. Do a front start and sprint forward across the ice. Execute the initial push of the start with your left leg.
6. Stop at the opposite sideboards, now stopping to the right, and prepare to skate backward.
7. Do a left-over-right backward crossover start and sprint backward to your original position.
8. Stop at the original sideboards using a one-foot backward snowplow stop with your left foot, and prepare to skate forward again.
9. Keep repeating the exercise. Each time you stop, alternate the stopping side and the stopping leg. This also means that you must alternate the leg that performs the initial thrust of the subsequent forward or backward start.
10. Repeat the exercise, but do a straight backward start each time you begin skating backward.
11. Alternate straight backward striding with weaving backward crossovers to sprint backward.

Variation:

Repeat this exercise, using whistle signals to command the stops and starts.

Exercise 4

The following exercises are diagrammed in Figure 9.14. All are variations of the same pattern.

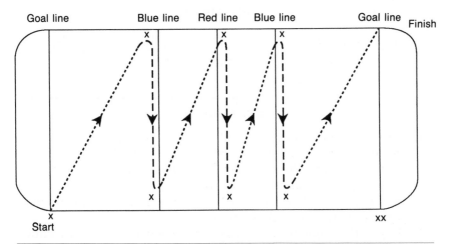

Figure 9.14 Stops and starts, alternating forward and backward skating.

1. Start from one corner of the rink with a front start. Sprint forward diagonally across the ice to the blue line at the opposite sideboards; stop.
2. Execute a straight backward start and sprint backward along the blue line across the ice; stop.
3. Execute a front start and sprint forward, diagonally across the ice to the center red line at the opposite sideboards; stop.
4. Execute a straight backward start and sprint backward along the red line across the ice; stop.
5. Execute a front start and sprint forward diagonally across the ice to the blue line at the opposite sideboards; stop.
6. Execute a straight backward start and sprint backward along the blue line across the ice; stop.
7. Execute a front start and sprint forward diagonally across the ice to the opposite corner; stop.
8. Repeat the exercise, starting from that corner. Stop to the other side and use the other leg to execute the initial thrust of each start.
9. Alternate straight backward striding with weaving backward crossovers to sprint backward.

Variations:

1. Repeat the exercise, now doing backward crossover starts.
2. Repeat the exercise, now skating forward all the time. Use hockey stops and crossover starts throughout.

Exercise 5

1. Repeat Exercise 4, but start out from one corner skating backward. Start with a straight backward start and sprint backward diagonally across the ice to the first blue line at the opposite sideboards. Stop, using a one-foot backward snowplow stop.
2. Execute a forward start, using the stopping leg of the backward stop as the initial pushing leg of the forward start, and sprint forward along the blue line back across the ice; stop.
3. Continue in this manner until you reach the finishing corner as described in Exercise 4.

Variation:

Repeat Exercise 5, but start backward using backward crossover starts.

Chapter

10

TURNS

Turns—the ability to change the direction you are facing while maintaining speed—are critical to a player's maneuverability. In game situations players must be able to turn around instantly and without warning, maintaining speed all the while. The most frequently used turns involve a change of feet during the turn with an accompanying rotation of the entire body.

Basic Principles of All Turns

Like all skating maneuvers, turns utilize the edges of the blades. Even turns executed along a straight path should be performed on slight edges so that the skater will have traction in the ice.

In order to execute a turn, the upper body and the hips must rotate to face the intended line of travel *before* you change feet. Your feet step around *after* your body has arrived. If you try to change feet before turning your body you will end up stepping sideways across the line of travel.

To stay in the play, players must maintain speed before and during the turn and be able to accelerate on completing it. Many learning players perform a snowplow skid just before turning. This slows them down and also prevents them from turning properly. A turn must be executed like a small jump, in order to release the body weight from the ice and facilitate the turn. A scraping sound just before turning means you have slowed yourself down and have also affected your ability to turn properly. It is better to hop or jump into the turn than to slow down.

After a turn, you must accelerate; consequently you must finish the turn prepared to thrust powerfully and rapidly. Too many players turn and then coast. Once you have turned, you must go! Otherwise you will be out of the play.

Turns must be mastered skating straight ahead and also on a curve or circle. When turning on a straight line, use slight edges. When turning on a curve or circle, use deeper edges. The deeper the edges and greater the knee bend, the sharper the curve.

Whether on the attack or on defense, whenever possible, turn so that you face the action. Turning with your back to the play limits your effectiveness. Try to master all turns in this chapter to develop quickness and agility.

When turning while skating a curve the body sometimes rotates in the same direction as the curve and sometimes in the opposite direction. Likewise, sometimes you will be required to turn with the upper body facing into the curve or circle, or sometimes facing out of the curve (the latter is the case when the turns are done on outside edges).

For example, when turning around and switching from LFI to RBI, you skate a clockwise curve and your body rotates clockwise as well. When switching from RFI to LBI, you skate a counterclockwise curve and your body rotates counterclockwise. But when turning around and switching from LBI to RFI, you skate a counterclockwise curve, but your body rotates clockwise. And when turning around from RBI to LFI, you skate a clockwise curve while your body rotates counterclockwise.

You may also be called upon to turn from backward to forward in the following ways: LBI to RFO, RBI to LFO, LBO to RFI, or RBO to LFI. In these four turns, the *direction of the curve* changes when you turn around from backward to forward.

Remember: The key factor in executing any turn is to turn your head, shoulders, chest, and hips all the way around *before* changing feet or trying to step in the new direction!

Keep shoulders level, back straight, and head up for all turns. If your leading shoulder drops or if you slump forward or put your head down you may lose balance and speed.

Practice all turns in both directions and give special attention to the weaker side. To practice a turn in the direction opposite the one described, mirror the instructions given.

Turning From Forward to Backward on a Straight Line or Curve

This turn is a two-step turn which is sometimes called a Mohawk turn. The turn is described for skating a straight line and for turning to your right. Remember: Turn your head, shoulders, chest, and hips *before* turning and stepping onto the new skating foot.

Step 1

1. Skate forward on a slight left inside edge. Hold your right foot behind you and off the ice (Figure 10.1a). Rotate your head, shoulders, chest, and hips clockwise as in Figure 10.1b.
2. Bring your free (right) foot close to your skating (left) foot, turning the free foot to point backward (toe facing opposite the *intended* line of travel) as it draws near the skating foot.

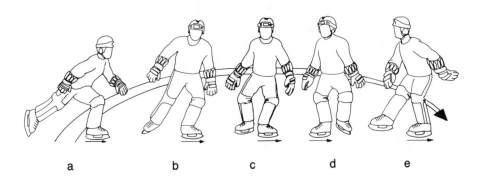

a   b   c   d   e

Figure 10.1   Turn from forward to backward (Mohawk turn) on a straight line or curve.

Your feet will be in an open, exaggerated V position, with heels close together and toes pointing in almost opposite directions (Figure 10.1c). Note that your right foot is still off the ice.

3. Keep rotating your head, shoulders, chest, and hips until your hips and free foot have turned 180 degrees to face fully backward. It is essential that the foot about to skate point backward (toe facing opposite the intended line of travel) before it takes the ice. The foot cannot touch down facing backward unless your hips have already turned to face backward.

Step 2

1. Now change feet; place your right foot (slight inside edge) on the ice, lift your left foot, and skate backward. As you change feet lift your left foot immediately. Otherwise it will be hit by the right one as the right foot takes the ice (Figure 10.1d).
2. You have completed the turn. Your right foot is now the skating foot and your left is the free foot.
   Thrust with your right leg, using the backward C-cut thrust against the inside edge of the right skate, and skate backward onto your left foot (Figure 10.1e).
3. Execute a series of backward C-cut pushes and sprint backward.

POINTS TO REMEMBER

- Keep your feet close together while switching them. If they are far apart, your weight will be split between your feet and the pushing foot will not be centered under your body. As a result you will lose thrusting power and speed. As always a thrust is effective only when the body weight is totally over the thrusting leg.
- The use of slight inside edges is imperative when performing the turn. Without the edges to grip the ice, the necessary prerotation of the upper body would also rotate the skating foot, causing it to slide and scrape sideways on the ice.
- To execute this turn on a curve or circle, each skate glides on a deep inside edge. Your body must rotate so that your chest faces toward the center of the curve.

Turning From Backward to Forward on a Straight Line or Curve

Hockey players often have to turn from backward to forward and immediately accelerate. Numerous plays demand this move. For example, after backing up with the puck, a player must turn forward to carry the puck toward the offensive zone. Or, defenders must accelerate as they turn from backward to forward to cut off attacking opponents.

There are two methods of executing this critical turn. One involves using an open (V or Mohawk) turn and the other a backward crossover prior to turning. Either can be performed on a straight line of travel (180 degrees), on a diagonal line of travel (for cutting an opponent off at the boards), or on a curve. Both methods should be practiced as straight line, diagonal, and circle turns.

The Open (V or Mohawk) Turn

This is a two-step turn. It is described for skating a straight line and for turning to your right.

Step 1

1. Skate backward on a slight LBI. Hold your right foot in front of you and off the ice (Figure 10.2a).
2. Rotate your head, shoulders, chest, and hips clockwise (to the right; Figure 10.2b) and bring your free (right) foot close to your skating (left) foot, turning the free foot to point forward, toe facing the *intended* line of travel as it draws near your skating foot. Your feet will be in an open, exaggerated V position, with toes pointing in almost opposite directions (Figure 10.2c). Note that your right foot is still off the ice.
3. Keep rotating your head, shoulders, chest, and hips until your hips and free foot have turned 180 degrees to face fully forward, *toward your intended line of travel.* Your right foot is still off the ice (Figure 10.2d).
4. It is essential that the toe of the foot about to skate point forward along the new line of travel before it takes the ice. Remember: The foot cannot touch down facing forward until your hips have turned to face forward.

Step 2

1. To complete the turn, change feet; place your right foot (slight

inside edge) on the ice, and skate forward on your right foot (Figure 10.2e).

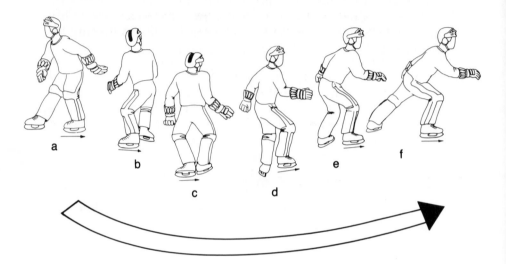

Figure 10.2   Turn from backward to forward (Mohawk turn) on a straight line or curve.

2. As you step forward onto your right skate, thrust your left leg against the left inside edge to accelerate (Figure 10.2f). Sprint forward.

POINTS TO REMEMBER

•   Keep your feet close together while changing feet in order to have your body weight totally over the pushing leg.

- To accelerate as you exit from the turn use the V position of the feet as though you were doing a front start (chapter 8) and sprint forward.
- The basic difference between turning on a curve and on a straight line is in the depth of the edges. When executing this turn on a curve or circle, each skate must glide on a deep inside edge. Your body must rotate so that your chest faces the center of the curve. See Figure 10.3 for a guide to forward and backward turns on a circle. See Figures 10.4a and b for a guide to turning forward on a line diagonal to your original line of travel.

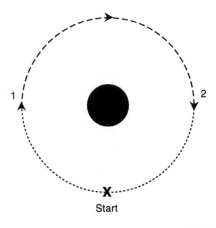

Start

Figure 10.3   Turn from forward to backward on a circle—body rotation with chest facing toward center of circle: Skate forward on LFI from X; turn backward at 1; skate backward on RBI; turn forward at 2, skating forward on LFI to X.

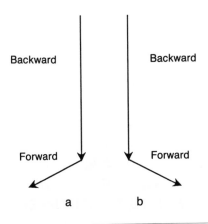

Figure 10.4   Turn from backward to forward on a diagonal line: (a) turning to left or (b) to right.

The Backward Crossover Turn

This turn is described for skating a clockwise circle or curve. Your upper body must rotate counterclockwise (to the left); your chest must face toward the center of the circle in preparation for turning. This is a three-step turn.

Step 1

1. Skate backward with your weight on your left outside edge. Hold your right foot in front of you and off the ice. (Figure 10.5a).
2. Prepare to do a backward crossover; start rotating your upper body as described (i.e., to the left).

Step 2

1. Do a right-over-left backward crossover. When your right foot takes the ice, it should be on the RBI (Figures 10.5b and c). You will still be skating backwards.
2. While on the RBI continue rotating your head, shoulders, chest, and hips counterclockwise. Your chest must face toward the center of the curve as your body rotates (see Figure 10.5c).
3. Bring your free (left) foot close to your skating (right) foot, and turn the free foot to point forward (toe facing the intended line of travel) as it draws near the skating foot. Your feet will be in an exaggerated V, almost a spread-eagle position. Note that your left foot is still off the ice (Figure 10.5d).
4. Keep rotating your head, shoulders, chest, and hips until your hips and free foot have turned 180 degrees to face fully forward. It is essential that the toe of the free foot point forward before it takes the ice. Remember: The foot will not face forward until your hips have done so.

Step 3

1. To complete the turn, change feet; place your left foot on the ice , lift your right foot immediately, and skate forward on the LFI (Figure 10.5e).
2. As you step forward onto the LFI, thrust your right leg against the right inside edge to accelerate from the turn.
3. Use the V position of the feet as in a front start, and sprint forward pushing powerfully and rapidly.

Variation:

Do the same turn, but after turning, skate forward on a diagonal to your original line of travel.

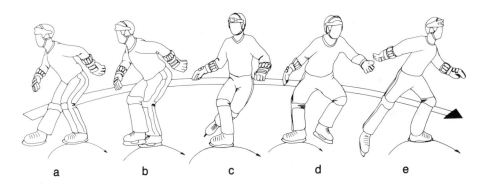

a   b   c   d   e

Figure 10.5   Turn from backward to forward using a backward cross-over prior to turning.

POINTS TO REMEMBER

- Use both pushes of the backward crossover to accelerate *into* the turn.
- Keep your feet close together while changing feet. If they separate, your body weight will be split between your feet rather than centered over the thrusting leg, resulting in a loss of thrusting power.
- Keep knees bent and stay low while you turn. Straightening up will throw your momentum upward, causing a loss of speed.

- While thrusting from backward to forward and during the initial forward strides, use the V foot position with your body weight projected low and well forward (as in the front start) to accelerate.

Exercises for Improving Turns

The following exercises are examples of the many available. They are divided into circle, straight line, pattern and defensive turn exercises.

Mirror the instructions to practice turns in the opposite direction.

Circle Exercises

Exercise 1

This exercise is described for skating a counterclockwise circle.

1. Skate forward crossovers on a circle. Skate onto the RFI. Rotate your head, shoulders, chest, and hips counterclockwise 180 degrees, chest facing the center of the circle.
2. Turn backward onto the LBI.
3. With your left (outside) leg, thrust (backward C-cut push) against the inside edge of the left skate and proceed to do a series of left-over-right backward crossovers on the same counterclockwise circle.
4. On the last crossover cross your left foot over in front of your right and skate onto the LBI. Pick up your right foot.
5. Rotate your head, shoulders, chest, and hips clockwise 180 degrees.
6. Turn forward and change feet, stepping onto the RFI.
7. Keep repeating the sequence, skating a continuous circle of forward to backward and backward to forward turns.

Exercise 2

This exercise is described for skating a counterclockwise circle. The first turn demands body rotation with the chest facing *away* from the center of the circle, while the second turn demands body rotation with the chest facing *toward* it. A backward crossover is incorporated into the exercise.

1. Skate forward crossovers on a circle.
2. When your weight is on the LFO, rotate your head, shoulders, chest, and hips clockwise so that your chest faces away from the center of the circle. Turn backward, landing on two feet. (This turn is like a small jump in that both feet come off the ice slightly to turn.)
3. With your left (outside) leg, thrust (backward C-cut push) against the inside edge of the left skate and proceed to do a series of left-over-right backward crossovers on the same counterclockwise circle.
4. As you begin the last crossover, rotate your head, shoulders, chest, and hips clockwise, facing the center of the circle. As you cross your left foot in front of the right and land on the LBI, continue rotating your upper body to the right until it has turned 180 degrees to face fully forward.
5. Now step forward onto the RFI. Push with your left leg, thrusting against the inside edge of your left skate to accelerate. Keep accelerating with the original right-over-left forward crossovers.
6. Repeat the sequence, skating a continuous circle in the same direction.

Exercise 3 (The Windmill)

This exercise is described for skating a counterclockwise circle (Figure 10.6). It is excellent for improving balance, agility, and

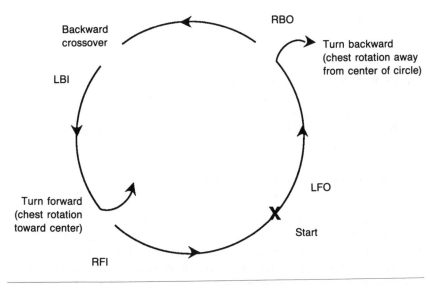

Figure 10.6 Pattern of the windmill exercise.

mobility (BAM). The exercise consists of four steps performed with only one skate on the ice at a time. The body rotations are the same as for Exercise 2. To do the first turn, from forward to backward, the clockwise body rotation must turn your chest *away* from the center of the circle and on the second turn, from backward to forward, the clockwise body rotation must turn your chest into the circle.

Step 1

1. Skate forward crossovers on a circle. Skate onto the LFO, holding your right foot behind you and off the ice.
2. Rotate your head, shoulders, chest, and hips clockwise so that your chest faces away from the center of the circle (Figure 10.7a). Rotate until your head, shoulders, chest, and hips turn 180 degrees to face fully backward. At the same time bring your free (right) foot behind the heel of your left foot with your heel facing backward. In preparation for skating backward the heel of the free foot must face the intended line of travel while it is still off the ice.

Step 2

1. Change feet so you are now skating on the RBO (Figure 10.7b). Push with your left leg, driving it against its outside edge, as you change feet (Figure 10.7c).
2. Keep rotating your upper body clockwise. As you rotate, your head, shoulders, chest, and hips will face toward the center of the circle.

Step 3

1. Do a left-over-right backward crossover. Your left foot takes the ice on its LBI while your right foot thrusts (crossunder or scissor push) and then becomes the free leg (Figures 10.7d and e).
2. Keep rotating your head, shoulders, chest, and hips until your body has turned 180 degrees to face fully forward (Figure 10.7f). At the same time bring your free (right) foot close to your skating foot and turn it so your toe points forward as it draws near the skating foot. Your feet will be in an exaggerated V position in preparation for stepping forward.

Step 4

1. Step forward onto the RFI. Thrust your left leg against its inside edge as you step onto the right foot (Figure 10.7g).

Figure 10.7 Windmill exercise.

2. You have completed one sequence. To begin again, step onto the LFO and thrust from the inside edge of the right foot (Figure 10.7a).
3. Continue the sequence, skating a continous counterclockwise circle and always rotating your body clockwise.

As you become more proficient at the exercise, push harder, skate faster, and use deeper edges.

Straight Line Exercises

Exercise 1

Sprint forward from the goal line. At the first blue line, turn around, accelerate, and sprint backward to the center red line. At the red line, turn around, accelerate, and sprint forward to the far blue line. At the far blue line, turn around, accelerate, and sprint backward to the far goal line. Thrust and accelerate as you exit from each turn.

NOTE: Always turn your body toward the same side of the rink. In this way your turns will be in one direction skating up the ice, and in the opposite direction coming back down the ice when the sequence is reversed.

Variations:

1. Do the same exercise on whistle signals.
2. Do the above exercises on a straight line, using two-foot turns as described in Exercise 2 of the Circle Exercises.

Exercise 2: Jump Turns

The purposes of this exercise are to learn to rotate your body 180 degrees as well as to improve balance when recovering from situations that involve jumping.

1. Skate forward on a straight line.
2. On a whistle signal, jump up and turn around 180 degrees in the air. Land backward on two feet. Skate backward.
3. On the next whistle, jump up, turn 180 degrees in the air, and land forward on two feet. Skate forward.

NOTE: When landing, be sure your back is straight and both blades are in complete contact with the ice. If your heels lift up you will pitch forward over your toes. Also, be sure to flex your knees deeply to cushion the jolt of landing. Remember: You cannot turn around without a 180-degree rotation of the upper body prior to turning.

Pattern Exercises

Exercise 1: "N" Drill

Refer to Figure 9.14 in chapter 9 (p. 161). Perform turns at the X in Figure 9.14. In this drill the turns executed on each length of the ice should be done facing the same sideboards.

1. Start in one corner of the rink and skate forward diagonally across the ice to the sideboards at the first blue line. At the

boards, turn around and skate backward along the blue line across the ice to the opposite sideboards. The turn from front to back is a jumping, two-foot turn with your chest facing toward the sideboards (away from the center of the curve).

2. After skating backward across the ice, turn around and skate forward diagonally across the ice to the sideboards at the center red line. The turn from back to front is a backward crossover turn with your chest facing toward center ice (toward the center of the curve). Do not decelerate to execute the turn, and accelerate as you exit from it.

3. Using the two-foot turn, turn around at the boards and skate backward across the ice along the red line.

4. Using the backward crossover turn, turn around at the boards and skate forward diagonally across the ice to the next blue line.

5. Using the two-foot turn, turn around at the boards and skate backward across the ice along the blue line.

6. Using the backward crossover turn, turn around at the boards and skate forward to the opposite goal line.

7. Using the two-foot turn, turn around at the boards and skate backward along the goal line to the new start position (XX). Repeat, arranging the drill so that the turns face the same sideboards; the turns will be executed in *your* opposite direction (right as opposed to left, or vice-versa).

Exercise 2

This exercise is diagrammed in Figure 10.8. Be sure to accelerate from all turns.

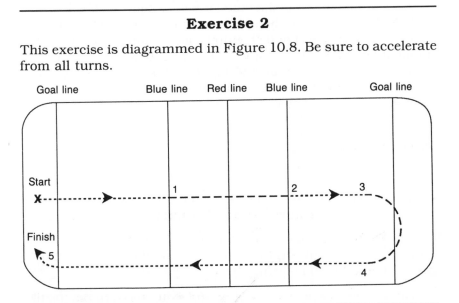

Figure 10.8   Turn exercise.

1. Start from the goal line. Skate forward to the first blue line (1) and turn, facing one predetermined sideboards. Skate backward to the far blue line (2).
2. At the far blue line, turn, facing the same sideboards, and skate forward to the end face-off circle (3). As you reach it turn backward, facing the net; immediately execute a backward crossover and then a turn forward (4). Skate forward, returning back up the ice to point 5.
3. Repeat the exercise, all turns facing the other sideboards.

Exercise 3: Turns Along the Blue Line

In this exercise only one foot is on the ice and your upper body is perpendicular to your line of travel all the time. You will continuously turn and step from forward to backward and backward to forward, executing the turns as quickly as possible. Your upper body must face the same end of the rink throughout the exercise.

1. Start from the sideboards at the blue line. Glide forward along the blue line on your left foot, keeping your right foot off the ice. Rotate your upper body so that your chest faces the endboards to your right.
2. Change feet so that you glide backward on your right foot. Glide backward along the blue line for a very short distance, keeping your left foot off the ice. Keep your upper body positioned so that your chest still faces the same endboards.
3. Change feet and glide forward along the blue line on your left foot again for a very short distance, keeping your right foot off the ice. Maintain the same upper body position.
4. Keep turning and changing feet—left foot on the ice when gliding forward and right foot on the ice when gliding backward—until you reach the opposite side of the rink.
5. Repeat the exercise, gliding forward on your right foot and backward on your left.

You may find it helpful to do the exercise holding a hockey stick horizontally in both hands to assist in positioning your upper body toward the endboards. Keep the stick parallel to the endboards you are facing.

Be sure to push from one foot to the other instead of just stepping. Remember that to push you must dig in the inside edge, bend your knees, and have your body weight situated over the thrusting leg.

Defensive Turn Exercises

The remaining three exercises simulate situations where the defender is skating backward but must turn and skate forward to cut off an opponent.

Exercise 1

1. Using a backward crossover start, start from the goal line and skate straight backward to the first blue line.
2. At the blue line, turn forward, facing the sideboards to your left. Use the open (Mohawk) turn. As soon as you have turned forward, accelerate by thrusting as in the front (V) start and sprint forward on a diagonal path to reach the sideboards at the center red line (Figures 10.9a, b, and c).
3. Repeat the exercise, this time turning to face the sideboards to your right.

a

b

c

Figure 10.9 Turn to the left from backward to forward (Mohawk or V turn) to cut off an opponent.

Figure 10.10 Turn to the right from backward to forward (backward crossover turn) to cut off an opponent.

Exercise 2

This exercise is described for turning from backward to forward to your right. Start in the same manner as in Exercise 1. This time, however, when you reach the first blue line use a backward crossover move preceding the turn from backward to forward, then turn forward facing the sideboards to your right. As soon as you have turned forward, accelerate by thrusting as in the front start and sprint forward on a diagonal path to reach the sideboards at the center red line (Figures 10.10a through g).

Repeat the exercise, this time turning to face the sideboards to your left.

Exercise 3

Start in the same manner as described in Exercise 1 and skate straight backward to the first blue line.

At the blue line, turn forward using the open (Mohawk) turn and skate forward along the same straight line of travel. As you turn, accelerate by thrusting as in the front start. Sprint the length of the ice. Alternate the turning side on each repetition.

Variation:

Repeat Exercise 3, but do a backward crossover prior to turning from backward to forward. Be sure to use both pushes of the backward crossover to accelerate into the turn.

Chapter

11

AGILITY

Agility often marks the difference between a mediocre hockey player and a star. It provides the wherewithal to outfox an opponent or keep a foe at bay; to execute a wide range of moves with dazzling speed and mobility; to dominate the action. Agile hockey players can regain their feet and get back into the play quickly after a fall or unexpected body check. Denis Savard exemplifies agility on ice.

The skills and exercises in this chapter are a guide to improving your agility. Goalies too should practice them diligently, because agility is a key to a goalie's success in the nets. The Pivot (tight turn) is presented first, followed by other agility moves and exercises. Keep in mind, however, that several moves already covered in this book might also fall under the category of agility maneuvers.

The Pivot (Tight Turn)

The pivot is a forward skating move in which the player executes a tight turn and emerges from it, *still skating forward*, but in a new direction (Figure 11.1). It is an important hockey move, because when properly executed it helps elude the opponent. The object is to make a very tight turn skating forward and when the pivot is completed to skate rapidly forward in *another* direction. The move

Figure 11.1   The pivot (tight turn).

is also used when trying to "bull" around a defending player—pushing that player away while cutting around him.

The pivot is initiated with both skates on the ice. It incorporates a forward C-cut. While the skating (inside) foot glides on a strong outside edge the outside leg executes a C-cut push. The C-cut enables you to accelerate through the first half of the pivot.

The maneuver depends on using deep edges on both the gliding and pushing skates, a hard-driving C-cut push with the thrusting leg, and proper weight distribution over the blades (your weight must be over the back halves of the blades). The depth of the edges and the downward pressure of the body weight over them determine the sharpness of the turn.

NOTE: The tighter the pivot the more important to have the body weight over the back halves of the blades. Weight on the fronts of the blades will cause a skid.

The pivot is a two-step maneuver. It is described here for turning to the left (counterclockwise).

Skate forward to a pylon and prepare to pivot around it in a counterclockwise direction (Figure 11.2a).

Step 1

1. At the pylon, dig in the edges of both skates and bend your knees. Your inside (left) foot is on a strong outside edge and your outside (right) foot is on a strong inside edge. Your body weight must be over the outside leg as it thrusts.
2. Thrust the outside leg against the inside edge, using the C-cut push. Turn sharply around the pylon. Thrust with the entire blade length; start with the heel of the inside edge and finish with the toe of the inside edge. During the push, transfer your

Figure 11.2   Performing the pivot: (a) preparation; (b) chest faces toward or (c) away from center of curve; (d) hips continuously face direction of travel; (e,f) emerge from pivot with crossover, skate forward.

weight onto the LFO of your gliding foot. Figure 11.2b demonstrates step 1 performed with the chest facing into the curve. Figure 11.2c demonstrates step 1 with the chest facing out of the curve.

3. Keep your hips continuously facing the circular direction of travel during the maneuver (Figure 11.2d). If your hips don't turn continuously you can't pivot quickly.

Step 2

1. At a certain point in the pivot (approximately halfway through), do a crossover, accelerating with the crossunder (scissor) push (Figure 11.2e). If the crossunder push is eliminated, you will be unable to come out of the turn at speed. Execute the crossunder push powerfully and rapidly. Land the crossover on the front part of its inside edge for quick acceleration.
2. Emerge from the pivot skating forward toward the direction from which you came (Figure 11.2f).
3. Practice the pivot in a clockwise direction. Your right foot is now the inside foot and glides on its outside edge, and your left foot is now the outside foot and cuts the C-cut push with its inside edge.

The pivot can be done either with your outside shoulder leading and your chest facing toward the center of the circle (Figure 11.2b), or with your inside shoulder leading and your chest facing away from the center of the circle (Figure 11.2c). Practice both positions. Regardless of the position, keep your shoulders as level as possible. If you drop your inside shoulder you may lose your balance.

The pivot can be used as a full-circle (360-degree) turn, a three-quarter-circle (270-degree) turn, a half-circle (180-degree) turn, or any part of a circle the situation demands. Players who master this maneuver have a major advantage over their opponents.

Pivot Exercises

In pivot exercises hold the hockey stick with both hands and keep the stick blade on or close to the ice. This prepares you to control the puck while pivoting. Practice all pivot exercises first without a puck and later with one.

Exercise 1

Pivot 360 degrees around a series of pylons. After pivoting half way around each pylon execute a crossover and the accompanying crossunder (scissor) push to accelerate through the second half of the pivot (the exit from the pivot). Skate to the next pylon and pivot around it in the opposite direction. Alternate the direction of the pivot at each pylon and stay as close to each pylon as possible (Figure 11.3).

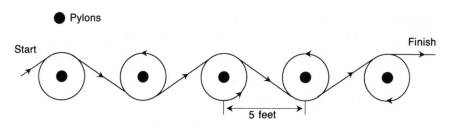

● Pylons

Start

Finish

|← 5 feet →|

Figure 11.3   360-degree pivots around pylons.

Exercise 2

Practice 270-degree pivots around a pylon. Skate forward and pivot 270 degrees around a pylon. After the pivot, skate back in the direction from which you just came. As in all pivots, approximately halfway through use a crossover move with crossunder push to pick up speed.

Exercise 3

Set up pylons and practice 270-degree pivots in a figure-eight pattern (Figure 11.4).

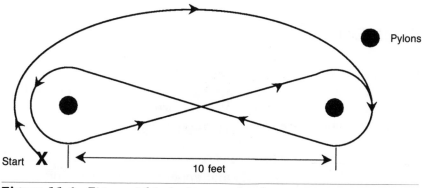

● Pylons

Start **X** |← 10 feet →|

Figure 11.4   Figure-eight pivots around pylons.

Exercise 4

Sprint forward from the goal line, staying just to the left of the midline of the rink. Just before reaching the center red line, pivot, turning toward the sideboards on your left. *Do not* cross the midline of the rink prior to pivoting. Stay inside (toward the center of the ice) the face-off dots on the left side of the rink as you pivot, cross over, and skate forward to the finish point on the goal line (Figure 11.5).

Repeat the drill, now starting just to the right of the midline of the rink and pivoting to your right.

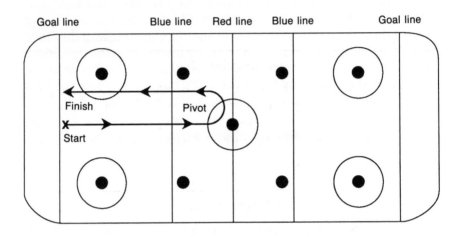

Goal line   Blue line   Red line   Blue line   Goal line

Figure 11.5 Pivot exercise.

POINTS TO REMEMBER

- Keep the pivot as tight as possible.
- Knee bend, edge depth, hip and upper body rotation, and speed determine the tightness of the pivot.
- During the pivot, keep your inside shoulder slightly higher than your outside shoulder for balance.

Exercise 5

"Bulling" around an opposing player: As the puck carrier skates down the ice, an opposing player may try to take the attacker out of the play by pushing the attacker toward the boards. If the attacker uses the pivot in such a situation it is possible to cut around the defender. To practice this maneuver, team up with another player; one acts as the attacker, the other as the defender.

Skate forward to the blue line, staying abreast of each other. At the blue line the defender should try to push the attacker toward the boards, using the inside shoulder to push the attacker.

To counter this move the attacker should get into position to pivot around the defender with the inside shoulder leading and the chest facing away from the center of the curve (away from the defender). The attacker uses the inside shoulder and back to push against the defender while executing the pivot. Deep edges and a strong C-cut thrust with the outside leg are essential (Figure 11.6).

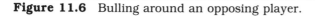

Figure 11.6   Bulling around an opposing player.

As the attacker the aim is to use the pivot to cut in front of the defender and then execute a crossover (with the accompanying crossunder push) to accelerate around and get away from the defender.

Practice bulling while holding the hockey stick with just the top hand and shielding a puck as you bull around the defender.

Keep shoulders level throughout the pivot. If you drop the inside shoulder, the defender has only to back away for the attacker to land on the ice!

Exercise 6

Follow the N pattern diagrammed in Figure 9.14 (p.161, chapter 9) for an additional pivot drill. Skate forward from a corner of the rink and follow the pattern, pivoting at each X.

There are many variations and patterns for practicing pivots. The better the skater, the more challenging the exercises should be.

Exercises for Improving Agility

360-Degree Spin-Around

A hard check can often send a player reeling to the ice. Some skaters manage to stay on their feet and retain their composure after such a check, while others end up out of the play. This exercise attempts to recreate such a situation and, by practice, teaches you to keep your balance and recover quickly when it happens.

The spin-around involves making a 360-degree rotation as rapidly as possible. It is executed with both feet on the ice during the spin.

1. Skate forward. Pretend you've just been hit with a hard check and spin around completely so that after the spin you are facing forward again.
2. When spinning, stay on the flats of the blades, your weight on the balls of your feet. Do not try to dig in the edges to spin around. If an edge catches the ice you will have difficulty making a rapid spin.
3. Try to spin around in one continuous motion, although the turn is actually a combination of two turns: a forward-to-backward turn and a backward-to-forward turn.
4. The immediate concern after coming out of the spin is rapid acceleration. When you complete the spin-around and are facing forward again, you must dig into the ice with the inside edge of your back foot, and with your weight over your back leg thrust off powerfully and sprint back to the action.
5. Keep the hockey stick on or close to the ice as you spin around, holding the stick with both hands. Bring the stick around with you so it remains in front of you and close to the ice as you come out of the spin. A need to swing the stick high into the air as you spin is a sign of poor upper body control and poor stability. It also raises your center of gravity. These factors affect balance, speed, and recovery time.

Variation:

Practice the 360-degree spin-around in both directions. Then practice spinning around on whistle signals. On the first signal, spin around 360 degrees in one direction, and on the next whistle, spin around 360 degrees in the other direction. Alternate directions to develop both rotations and to avoid dizziness. The exercise can also be done spinning around the near blue line, center red line, and far blue line.

Inside Edges Around Pylons

When performing this next exercise, remember that the gliding skate and leg always becomes the pushing skate and leg. Use each skate and leg to both glide (for curved direction) and thrust (for acceleration). Refer to Figure 11.7.

1. Start from one corner of the rink and skate forward to the first pylon. At the pylon, curve around it by gliding on the inside edge of your outside skate (45-degree angle of inside edge, knee bent, back straight, head up). Keep the other skate (the inside skate) off the ice and close to the gliding foot.
2. After curving halfway around the pylon, the gliding skate becomes the pushing skate. Thrust the pushing leg against the inside edge on which you have been gliding to accelerate from the glide, and sprint forward to the next pylon. Again, curve around the pylon by gliding on the inside edge of your outside skate, the other skate off the ice.
3. After curving halfway around the pylon, thrust the pushing leg against the inside edge on which you have been gliding to accelerate and sprint forward to the next pylon.
4. Continue skating to and curving around each pylon until you reach the opposite corner of the rink.
5. Repeat, skating backward. Each push will be the backward C-cut push.

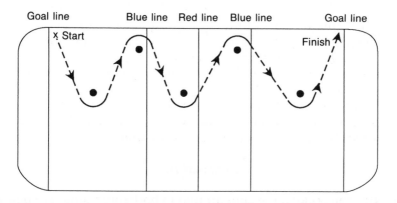

Figure 11.7   Edges around pylons.

Outside Edges Around Pylons

Perform the previous exercise forward and backward, but curve halfway around each pylon by gliding on the outside edge of the inside skate, with the outside skate off the ice. At this point do a crossover. Thrust against the outside edge of the skate on which you have been gliding. This push is the crossunder (scissor) push of forward and backward crossovers. Cross the outside skate over to take the ice on its inside edge. Use the crossunder push to accelerate from each glide.

Backward to Forward Turns Around Plyons

Skate the same pattern. Start out and skate backward. After curving backward halfway around the first pylon on the inside edge of your outside skate, turn forward quickly, thrust the pushing leg against the inside edge on which you've been gliding, and take three rapid forward strides toward the next pylon. After the third stride, turn backward quickly and skate backward the rest of the way to the pylon. Curve halfway around it on the inside edge of the outside skate, turn forward quickly, thrust the pushing leg against the inside edge on which you've been gliding, and take three rapid forward strides toward the next pylon. After the third stride, turn backward quickly and skate backward the rest of the way to the pylon. Continue this exercise until you reach the opposite corner of the rink.

All backward-to-forward turns must have the body rotation with your chest facing toward the center of the curve (facing the pylon).

As you curve around each pylon keep the inside skate off the ice and close to the gliding skate.

Many other variations of these exercises, incorporating turns (forward-to-backward and backward-to-forward), agility moves (such as 360-degree spin-arounds), full circles around pylons, and so on, can be designed.

Knee Drops

Players often must drop to their knees to block shots. They must be able to quickly return to an upright position and resume skating rapidly to stay with the action. Throughout this exercise keep your back straight and your head up.

1. One exercise to develop this skill is done standing in place on the ice. Hold a hockey stick horizontally and chest high in front

of you, arms outstretched. Keep the stick in this position during the entire drill. At no time should your hands, elbows, or stick touch the ice.

2. On a whistle signal, drop to both knees (Figure 11.8a).

3. On a second whistle, sit down to one side of your skates (Figure 11.8b). Be sure to practice sitting both ways. Here, too, most skaters favor one side over the other.

4. On a third whistle, get up on both knees (see Figure 11.8a). On a fourth whistle, get back up on your feet.

a   b   c

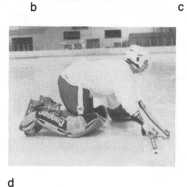

d

Figure 11.8   Knee drops: (a, b, c) correct form; (d) incorrect form.

Variations:

1. On the first whistle, drop to both knees simultaneously. On the next whistle, get up on your feet. Keep repeating as rapidly as possible.

2. This variation can be done skating forward or backward. On the first whistle, drop to both knees just as you did in the previous variation. On the second whistle, rise to your feet and get back into stride as quickly as possible.

3. This variation can be done skating forward or backward: On the first whistle drop to one knee, and on the second whistle get back up on your feet. Keep repeating this on alternating knees (Figure 11.8c).

4. Skate forward. On the whistle, drop to both knees. On the next whistle, get up, immediately turn backward, and skate backward rapidly. On the next whistle drop to both knees. On the next whistle, get up, immediately turn forward, and skate forward rapidly. This exercise can also be done dropping onto one knee. Alternate knees.

POINTS TO REMEMBER

- At no time should your hands, elbows, or stick touch the ice.
- When preparing to get up, center your support foot *directly underneath your body* with the entire blade length flat against the ice (see Figure 11.8c). If you place the front toe of the blade on the ice and lift your heel into the air you will not be able to get up.
- Keep your back straight and head up at all times. If your shoulders and head slump forward your weight will pitch over your toes and you will not be able to get up (Figure 11.8d).
- On all knee drops, drop gently so as not to injure your knees. Those with knee problems should not do knee drops.

Jumps Over Hockey Sticks

The ability to be airborne, land upright, and then sprint without losing stride is essential to agile hockey skating. You never know when you will be compelled to jump over a fallen player or be thrown into the air by an unexpected body check. Your ability to land and resume skating without breaking stride requires balance, body control, and stability. The use of the knees as shock absorbers is critical.

The following exercise is designed to improve balance and recovery capabilities in such situations.

1. Place a hockey stick horizontally over two pylons, the height of which is dependent on the size and ability of the skater.
2. Skate forward. Approach the stick gliding on two feet. Take off with both feet, lifting your knees simultaneously and jumping over the stick (Figure 11.9a). Land on both feet. Be sure to land with the entire blade lengths of both skates in contact with the ice. If you lift your heels as you land you will end up on your toes and may fall forward. If you land on your heels you will fall backward. On landing, flex your knees and keep your back straight, your shoulders back, and your head up. Advanced skaters can do this skating backward. Even more advanced skaters should jump, turn 180 degrees in the air, and land backward.
3. Do the same exercise, taking off from one foot and landing on the other (Figure 11.9b). Drive off with your back leg. Land on the opposite foot, keeping the original takeoff leg off the ice. Your body weight should be on the middle of the landing blade. Advanced skaters should also jump and land on the same foot.

a   b

Figure 11.9   Jumps over sticks.

To get the height necessary for clearing the stick, drive hard from the thrusting leg(s) to push your body into the air. Try not to slow down prior to jumping. You will acquire more height and clearance by accelerating into the takeoff. Immediately after landing resume skating rapidly, trying not to break stride.

Lateral Crossover Jumps

A player skating forward or backward on a straight line who wants to make a sudden sideways move to the boards or leap sideways over a fallen player may have to execute a lateral crossover jump. The move is similar to a crossover start. This exercise is similar to the crossover start exercise performed over hockey sticks (chapter 8). Here, only one stick is used.

1. Place the stick horizontally on top of two pylons, parallel to the direction of travel rather than across it. The height of the stick is dependent on the size and ability of the skater.
2. Skate forward until you are alongside and on the right side of the stick.
3. To leap over the stick do a lateral crossover jump by driving your inside (left) leg under your body. Push against the left outside edge to provide thrust through the leap, simultaneously crossing your outside (right) leg over the left. Drive your right knee and body weight sideways (to the left).
4. Leap over the stick so that your right foot lands on the other side of the stick on its inside edge, the skate blade almost parallel to the stick (Figures 11.10a and b). The landing skate must take the ice on its inside edge, nearly parallel to the stick. As soon as you land, pivot fully forward and use strong and rapid pushes to accelerate and sprint forward (see Figure 11.10c).
5. Do the exercise leaping over the stick from the other side (crossing left over right). More advanced skaters should do the same

a   b   c

Figure 11.10   Lateral crossover jump over stick.

from a backward skating position. When doing this, the leap will be a backward lateral crossover jump.

Dives

Hockey players quickly learn to expect the unexpected. You never know when you'll take a nose dive on the ice, but sooner or later you will. When it happens you must be able to regain your footing and immediately return to the action. Practicing this exercise will improve your ability to recover quickly from such falls.

1. Place a hockey stick horizontally on top of two pylons. Skate rapidly forward.
2. At the stick, belly flop with your hands flat out and your feet outstretched on the ice. Dive under the stick, trying not to knock it down (Figure 11.11).
3. After you have passed under the stick, get up as quickly as possible and resume skating with speed.

Figure 11.11   Dive under stick.

Variation:

Combine jumps and dives. Practicing them will improve the agility and quickness needed to jump up, land on your feet, dive, recover, and get back into stride with as little loss of time as possible.

Design a challenging pylon course. It is particularly difficult to dive, recover quickly, and jump over another stick that is only a few feet away from the stick under which you have just dived.

Defending Against a Check

Why are some hockey players able to remain in front of the net, unafraid, and withstand body checks that would stun other players?

The answer lies in the player's ability to use blade edges, knee bend, and body weight for maximum grip into the ice. Many players are unable to withstand checks because they do not achieve maximum traction and stability. Remember, once you've gotten to your desired position, your job is to stay on your feet and hold your ground.

As always, the more you dig in the blade edges and bend your knees, the more stable—and therefore stronger—you become. The best reply to a body check is to press down into the ice with as much force as you can apply to the inside edges and then push against the assaulting player. One of the most common errors is leaning away from a check. This pulls your edges, knees, and center of gravity up, and your strength can be likened to that of a feather in a hurricane.

If you are the player delivering the check, you need the same stability and must use your blade edges, knees, leg drive, and body weight to effectively hit the opposing player. If you don't, you will more than likely bounce off your opponent instead of taking him out of the play. To practice, concentrate on checking from the skates, legs, hips, and upper body.

1. Work with a partner. Each of you should check the other, shoulder to shoulder.
2. Both players must dig into the ice with the inside edge of the outside (back) foot (Figure 11.12) and with body weight over that leg, thrust against the edge with that leg. Try to move each other without giving up ice.

If you cannot stand your ground you are not digging in with enough inside edge, knee bend, or body weight. Strength on the ice depends on more than size.

Figure 11.12 Checking.

Tracking the Opponent

Pair up with another skater. Begin by skating as a forward while your partner acts as a defender. Using crossover leaps and sideways moves in alternating lateral directions, try to "deke" (fake) the defender. The defender should try to follow you, whichever way you go, without losing you (Figure 11.13a). Reverse roles and repeat the drill.

Also do this exercise with one of you skating forward and the other skating backward (Figure 11.13b).

a   b

Figure 11.13   Tracking the opponent.

Signal Exercise

This exercise combines many different skating skills, each performed in an unannounced sequence. The purpose is to develop agility and instantaneous response.

A particular signal will indicate a specific maneuver. On that signal, perform that maneuver as quickly as possible. The moves will be done one after the other, with no warning as to which will follow. A typical sequence might be as follows:

1. Skate forward.
2. Do crossover leaps to the right.
3. Skate backward.
4. Do crossover leaps to the left.
5. Pivot (tight turn) 360 degrees to the right.
6. Skate forward.
7. Drop to knees and get up.

8. Skate backward, drop to knees, and get up.
9. Pivot (tight turn) 360 degrees to the left.
10. Skate forward and stop.
11. Drop to knees, belly flop, get up on knees, and get up.
12. Skate forward, spin around 360 degrees, and keep skating forward.

The possible variations on this drill are endless. While working on technique, the skaters will also have fun!

Try a game of "follow the leader" using these variations.

Maneuvering the Puck With Your Skates

To the astonishment of fans, hockey players perform "miracles" by controlling the puck as easily with their skates as they do with their hockey sticks. To develop this skill, skate without a stick and control the puck with your skates. Try to move the puck from skate to skate; don't kick it out in front of you. Keep your head up, rather than looking down at the puck.

Other ways to develop this skill, using a puck and no sticks, include playing "one on one" with another player, "free for all" with several players, or even a regular "game" with fully equipped goalies. Remember: Everyone has only skates for shooting, passing, and puck control—no sticks!

Additional Agility Drills

Exercise 1

Note that the tightness of the pattern in this exercise requires deep edges, body control, and agility. Skate rapidly throughout. Refer to Figure 11.14.

1. Starting at X, sprint forward to point 1.
2. At 1, turn backward, facing into circle. Perform backward crossovers, left over right, to point 2.
3. Between 2 and 3, sprint backward (backward C-cuts).
4. From 3 to 4, perform backward crossovers, left over right.
5. At 4, turn forward, facing into circle.
6. From 4 to 1, sprint forward (forward stride).

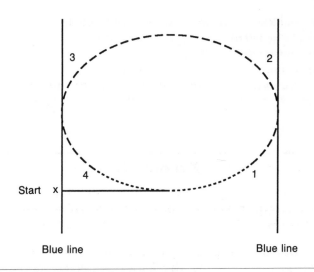

Figure 11.14   Agility exercise 1.

Variations:

1. Skate forward and use forward crossovers only.
2. Skate backward and use backward crossovers only.
3. Turn at 1 facing outside circle instead of inside.

Exercise 2

Refer to Figure 11.15.

1. Sprint forward from X to 1.

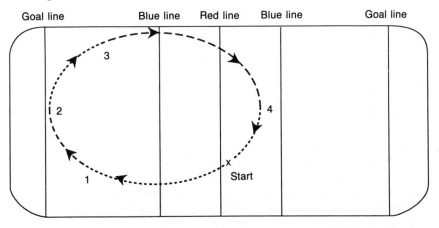

Figure 11.15   Agility exercise 2.

2. Turn backward at 1 and skate backward to point 2, using backward crossovers.
3. Turn forward at 2 and skate forward to point 3, using forward crossovers.
4. Turn backward at 3 and skate backward to point 4.
5. At point 4, turn forward and skate to X, using forward crossovers.

Exercise 3

Follow the circular patterns shown in Figure 11.16. The tightness of the pattern requires deep edges, body control, and agility. Skate rapidly.

1. Skate forward using the forward stride and forward crossovers.
2. Skate backward using the backward stride and backward crossovers.
3. Turn from forward to backward and backward to forward at blue and red lines.
4. Skate forward and pivot at the blue and red lines.

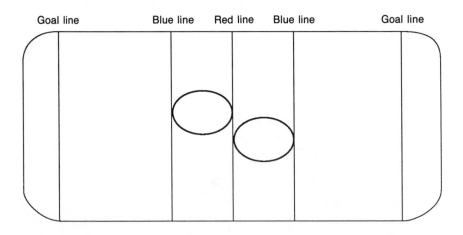

Figure 11.16   Agility exercise 3.

Exercise 4

Two players skate simultaneously, each starting from the boards directly opposite each other. Refer to Figure 11.17.

1. Skate forward from X to 1.

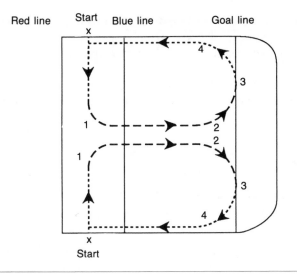

Figure 11.17 Agility exercise 4.

2. Turn backward at 1, facing outside the curve. Sprint backward to point 2.
3. Use backward crossovers from 2 to 3. Turn forward at 3, facing inside the curve.
4. Skate forward crossovers between 3 and 4. Sprint forward between 4 and X.

Exercise 5

Refer to Figure 11.18.

1. Sprint forward from X. Between 1 and 2 skate forward crossovers in and out of pylons.
2. At 3, jump over stick; at 4, dive under stick; and at 5 jump over stick again.
3. Between 6 and 7, perform 360-degree pivots. At 8, perform a lateral leap over stick.
4. Between 9 and 10, execute forward crossovers in and out of pylons. Turn backward at 11.
5. Between 11 and 15, perform backward crossovers in and out of pylons. Turn forward at 16.
6. From 16 to X, sprint forward. Perform a hockey stop at finish.

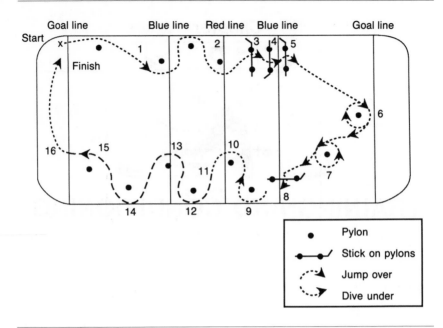

Figure 11.18 Agility exercise 5.

Chapter

12

TRAINING AND CONDITIONING

Hockey games are noted for their explosive bursts. Games are stressful work periods going almost nonstop for 2 to 3 hours with intensely demanding shifts lasting 45 to 80 seconds. Successful hockey players are finely trained and conditioned athletes, their muscles honed for power, speed, explosiveness, and agility, capable of working at peak performance even as fatigue sets in. Even if hockey players' skating techniques are good, they have little chance of reaching full potential in anything less than top shape.

Training and conditioning programs for hockey players are designed to improve flexibility, endurance, strength, power, speed, quickness, agility, and skating technique. Though the training techniques for each of these elements is different, all are interrelated and mutually dependent. For example, agility, which improves as the body becomes more flexible, also relies on endurance, because as fatigue sets in agility decreases. Power, too, is lost as players become fatigued. Awareness, visual acuity and reflexes are similarly affected.

Only in the last 15 years have coaches and sports scientists recognized that skating technique as well as quickness can be improved by training and conditioning. Before that it was thought that "you either can skate or you can't skate"; "you're either born to be fast or slow." Now we know the value of training in helping each athlete to reach his or her potential for speed.

There is no substitute for on-ice workouts. But a year-round training and conditioning program can help players skate faster than their current "fastest."

This chapter is an overview of the fundamentals of training and conditioning for hockey players. The exercises are just a sampling of those available. For more in-depth knowledge, study some of the extensive materials dealing specifically with this important topic; a few publications are mentioned at the end of this chapter. Also important in today's world of sports training are subjects such as visualization, mental training, positive self image, nutrition, fluid replacement, and rest, all of which you can also research.

Training and conditioning programs must fulfill the demands of the particular sport and the needs of the individual athlete. They should include enough variety to maintain a high level of interest.

Warm-Up and Cool-Down

As in other sports, every workout for hockey players should include a thorough warm-up and cool-down. This is accomplished by a program of light activity and stretching before and after workouts. Hockey is a sport of explosive motions and sudden changes of direction. Muscles cannot be called upon to perform these movements until they are readied for work. A warm-up routine prior to exercise or competition gradually brings the body from a state of rest to a state of readiness for work and reduces the likelihood of muscle and soft tissue injuries associated with sudden movement. Since it is easier to stretch muscles that are warm, before stretching it is beneficial to do some light warm-up activities such as slow skating, walking, or jogging. Five to 10 minutes of such activities are recommended.

For the cool-down phase (after exercise), a light skate or walk for 5 to 10 minutes followed by 10 to 15 minutes of stretching gradually brings the body from a state of work to a state of rest and prevents tightening of muscles.

Training for Flexibility

Flexibility is extremely important. Improving it brings several specific benefits to a hockey player's performance.

1. It contributes to speedier movement of the engaged muscle groups. As muscles and joints become more flexible they give less resistance to movement; this allows them to apply force

more rapidly and in a greater range of motion. As the speed of applied force increases, power also increases.

2. It increases agility, because muscles and joints can work more efficiently through their full range of motion.
3. It often delays the onset of fatigue. If there is less resistance by muscles and joints, less energy is needed to move through the full range of their motion. Thus activity can be continued longer before fatigue sets in.
4. It decreases the likelihood of muscle injury.

Flexibility is developed and maintained by means of an ongoing stretching program. Stretching serves three functions—first, to prepare the body for workout sessions; second, to develop body flexibility; and third, to cool down muscles after heavy exercise. Since ice time during the playing season is generally limited, off-ice stretching is advisable. During the off season players should participate in daily stretching sessions to improve or maintain flexibility.

Stretching exercises for both lower and upper body should be done for a minimum of 10 minutes before each workout and 10 to 15 minutes after each workout. Exercises should follow a procedure designed to gradually increase stretch. Dancers begin workouts stretching at a bar for about 30 minutes. They work slowly at first and gradually increase the demands on their muscles and joints. Plan your program with this in mind.

Remember, warm muscles are more flexible than cold ones. It is advisable to do other warm-up activities before and after stretching, always starting with gentle movement and gradually increasing demands on the muscles.

Stretching Procedure

Perform each stretch in a slow, sustained manner to the point where you feel light tension (stretching) in the stretched muscles. Hold this position for about 20 to 30 seconds. Relax and ease off for about 10 seconds. Then increase the stretch to a point of greater tension—but not pain. Hold this position for another 20 to 30 seconds. Bouncing can cause muscle injury and should be avoided.

The following stretching exercises are samples that can be incorporated into your routine. Vary them with other stretching exercises to make the workouts enjoyable.

For young people or people who are well conditioned or very flexible, these exercises should be quite safe. Those getting back into shape after an injury or a period of inactivity should be careful not to lock (hyperextend) joints or to put undue stress on the back, hips, neck, and knees.

Exercises for Improving Flexibility

Groin Stretches

1. Stand with your feet together, hands on your hips. Lower yourself by bending your right knee and stretching your left leg behind you. Keep your left foot on the floor. Lean forward while pushing hips downward and place one hand on each side of the forward foot. Repeat on the other leg (Figure 12.1a).
2. Sit on the floor with the soles of your feet touching. Place hands on ankles and slowly draw your feet toward your crotch. Press your elbows or forearms on the insides of your calves to push your knees toward the floor (Figure 12.1b).
3. Sit on the floor and spread your legs as wide apart as is comfortable. Place your hands on your legs or feet and reach your head toward the floor between your legs. Now place both hands on your right leg or foot and reach your head toward your right knee. Then do the same to your left (Figure 12.1c).

    Complete the exercise by moving your head through a slow circle, reaching it toward your right knee, between your legs, toward your left knee and, finally, sit up straight. Continue the

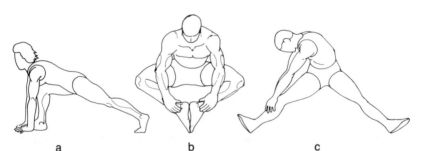

a   b   c

d   e

Figure 12.1   Groin stretches.

exercise in this circular manner, then repeat the circle in the other direction. Move in a slow circle and do not bounce. This exercise also loosens the waist and back muscles.

4. Stand with your feet about shoulder width apart and turned out, hands on hips. Keeping heels on the floor, squat by bending your knees, but do not bend beyond the point where your thighs are parallel to the floor. Straighten up and repeat (Figure 12.1d).

5. Kneel on your hands and knees. Now lift one leg off the floor and out to the side of your body. Straighten the lifted leg and lift it as high as is comfortable. Repeat with the other leg (Figure 12.1e).

Thigh (Quadriceps) Stretch

Stand on your right foot with your right hand against a wall for support. Lift your left foot and grasp it with your left hand. Point your left knee straight down toward the floor and draw the bent leg toward your buttocks. Feel the stretch in the upper front thigh (quadriceps). Do not try to pull the foot too close to buttocks as this will strain the knee. Repeat, standing on the left foot (Figure 12.2).

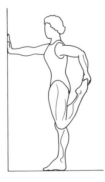

Figure 12.2   Thigh (quadriceps) stretch.

Hamstring Stretches

1. Stand with your feet 2 to 4 inches apart, knees straight but not locked. Bend over and reach both hands toward the floor, stretching one vertebra at a time. Hold stomach in. Never lock knees during this stretch. You do not need to completely straighten the knees to effectively stretch the hamstrings (Figure 12.3a).

2. Stand with your feet together. Lift one leg and place that foot on a bar or surface 3 to 4 feet off the floor. Keeping both knees bent, hug the lifted leg so that your waist and chest are close to the top of your thigh. Place your right hand on the right shin. Gradually straighten (but do not lock) your right leg, and simultaneously reach your head and chest toward your thigh. You do not need to completely straighten the knee to stretch properly. Repeat the exercise with the other leg lifted onto the bar. When you are on the ice the sideboards can be used as a bar (Figure 12.3b).

3. Kneel on your hands and knees and stretch one leg straight behind you on the floor. Lift this leg as high off the floor as is comfortable, keeping it straight. Repeat, stretching and lifting the other leg (Figure 12.3c).

4. Lie on your back and bring one knee up toward your chest, keeping the other leg on the floor. Grasp the bent knee with both hands and gently pull it toward your chin. Repeat the exercise with the other leg (Figure 12.3d).

a

b

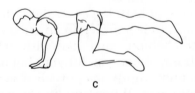

c

d

Figure 12.3 Hamstring stretches.

Calf/Achilles Tendon Stretches

1. Stand facing a wall, about 3 feet away from it. Place both palms against the wall. Bending your right knee, slide your left foot behind you until the left knee is straight. Keep both heels on the floor. Lean against the wall and gently press your weight down over your left heel to stretch the calf muscles. Switch legs (Figure 12.4a).

2. Sit on the floor with your legs stretched straight in front of you, feet together. Point your toes toward the ceiling. Place your hands on your feet and, keeping your knees straight, gently pull your toes toward you. Now bend forward and reach your head down toward your knees. Keep pulling your toes toward you as you lower your head. If you cannot grasp your feet, hold onto your calves or ankles (Figure 12.4b).

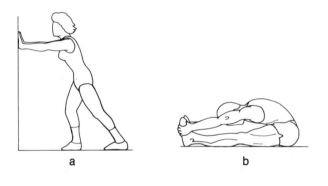

a   b

Figure 12.4   Calf/Achilles tendon stretches.

General Leg Stretches

1. Stand with your feet together, arms extended forward at shoulder height. Keeping both knees straight, lift the right leg up in front of you and move it toward your hands. Repeat the exercise, lifting your left leg (Figure 12.5a).

2. Stand in the same position. Keeping both knees straight, lift your right leg up in front of you. Circle your leg in an arc out to the side of your body, and then behind you. Finish with feet together. Repeat, lifting the left leg. When you lift your leg in front of you, you stretch the hamstring. When you lift it out to the side, you stretch the groin area. When you lift the leg behind you, you stretch the buttocks (Figure 12.5b).

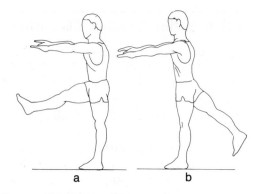

Figure 12.5 General leg stretches.

Back Stretches

1. Stand with feet apart and your arms extended over your head. Keep your knees straight, but not locked. Bend from the waist to reach both hands toward your right foot. Then make a large circle with your upper body by moving your arms to the left. Reach both hands toward your left foot. Continue the circle to the left until your hands are straight over your head. Then repeat the circle to the right (see Figure 12.6a). Do not bend backwards.

2. Stand with knees straight, but not locked, with your feet slightly apart. Extend both arms out to the sides of your body. Keep your hips facing straight ahead and slowly swing both arms horizontally to the left as far as is comfortable. Return your arms to the starting position and then slowly swing them horizontally to the right (Figure 12.6b).

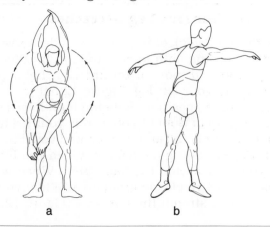

Figure 12.6 Back stretches.

Waist Stretches

1. Sit on the floor, legs straight out in front of you, hands on hips. Bend sideways from the waist and reach your left elbow toward the floor, keeping it as close to your left hip as possible. Sit straight up. Repeat the exercise, reaching your right elbow toward the floor, keeping it as close to your right hip as possible (Figure 12.7a).
2. Stand with your feet about shoulder width apart. Extend your arms straight overhead. Bend sideways at the waist and move your arms to the same side until you feel a comfortable stretch through your waist and side (Figure 12.7b).

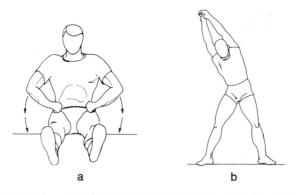

a   b

Figure 12.7   Waist stretches.

Shoulder and Arm Stretches

1. Hold your arms straight out to the sides of your body and move them in a circular pattern, 10 times in one direction and then 10 times in the opposite direction. Alternate between small and large circles (Figure 12.8a).
2. Put your arms behind your head. Grasp one elbow with the opposite hand and with that hand gently pull the elbow inward and down toward the back of your head (Figure 12.8b).

a   b

Figure 12.8   Shoulder and arm stretches.

Neck Stretches

1. Keeping chin pointed to chest, slowly roll head toward top of one shoulder. Hold the stretch at the top of shoulder. Still keeping chin to chest, gently slide head down and then up toward top of other shoulder. Hold the stretch. Repeat the sequence five times (Figure 12.9a).
2. Lie on your back, feet together and planted on the floor, knees up. Put your hands behind your neck. Using pressure from your hands, push neck and head gently forward to a comfortable stretch (Figure 12.9b).

a   b

Figure 12.9   Neck stretches.

Training for Endurance

Because of its intensity and duration, hockey requires that players possess *exceptional* endurance. Hockey combines explosive speed with powerful body checking, forceful maneuvering, and fighting for the puck. Sometimes bursts of speed are short and intense, with moments of slower skating or coasting in between. Other times players must skate all-out for entire shifts, almost without relief. Players must be conditioned so that they can recover completely from the previous shift during each brief rest period on the bench. Whatever the game situation, players must meet the demands with sufficient energy to give their all, even toward the end of an exhausting game.

The various demands of hockey require the development of different types of endurance, which we will refer to as wind (aerobic) endurance and explosive (anaerobic) endurance.

Wind (Aerobic) Endurance

Wind (aerobic) fitness is the base for all training and conditioning. Strength, power, and speed cannot be achieved unless the athlete has established a strong foundation of aerobic endurance.

When we breathe we take in oxygen, which the heart, lungs, and blood vessels transport to all parts of the body. Although the body has different mechanisms for producing energy, the most efficient, and therefore the most important, relies on the capabilities of the oxygen (aerobic) system to produce energy and the capabilities of the muscle cells to utilize that energy. Oxygen combines with nutrients in the cells to produce energy for work. Improving the aerobic system depends on increasing the efficiency of the heart so that it can pump more blood per beat. As the heart and circulatory system become more efficient, the player can work harder and longer with less stress before becoming fatigued and can recover more quickly to perform at top efficiency.

Aerobic training involves stressing the oxygen system by forcing the heart to beat at a higher rate than normal. The focus is to bring the heart rate up to 75% to 80% of its maximum during each workout of 30 to 50 minutes (alternating periods of work and rest). The heart rate during work periods should be brought to 160 to 180 beats per minute, depending on age. (The older the athlete, the lower the number of beats per minute.) The heart, lungs, and blood vessels will adapt to these greater demands and increase their capacity to transport oxygen. The muscles also adapt, and their ability to utilize energy improves.

Exercises for Improving Aerobic Endurance

Experts recommend that aerobic endurance workouts, which are performed at sub-maximal speeds, be done mostly off-ice so that the sub-maximal speeds do not negatively affect quickness, agility, and explosiveness on the ice. Off-ice activities that aid in developing aerobic endurance include distance and interval running (preferably on soft surfaces to lower the risk of injury), bicycling, dancing, aerobic dance, swimming, handball, racquet sports, basketball, soccer, gymnastics, and many other sports activities. Activity should be continuous for at least 30 minutes and performed three to four times a week.

Also helpful for endurance training are Rollerblades Training Skates (Figures 12.10a and b). Rollerblades Skates have wheels that simulate the ice skate blade. The use of edges, leg drive, and body weight are similar to skating on hockey skates so the skater, while focusing on endurance training, will also be using skating-specific muscles in skating-specific motions. The skater can practice skating technique while doing dryland training for endurance. When skating on Rollerblades Training Skates it is wise to wear protective equipment. Falls on hard pavement can hurt!

a   b

Figure 12.10   Rollerblade Training Skates.

The use of Rollerblades and the following on-ice drills are effective for improving aerobic endurance. But keep in mind that the submaximal leg speeds of these activities are not the leg speeds needed for hockey and may be counterproductive unless done in conjunction with quickness exercises (see section "Training for Quickness"). The weight of Rollerblades, for example, results in submaximal leg speeds.

Workouts with less rest than work increase endurance. They do not, however, improve skill or quickness, because fatigue limits the development of skill and quickness. Skating exercises in which the top priority is endurance must be used carefully for beginners, since they may sacrifice skill and technique development.

On-Ice Endurance Exercises

1. Skate continuous laps at half speed for 10 minutes. Skate easy and coast (the rest period) for 5 minutes. Repeat. Do this for 20 to 30 minutes.
2. Do the same, skating at half speed for 20 minutes and skating easy for 10 minutes.
3. Skate laps around the rink alternately skating slowly, moderately (3/4 speed), and short sprints (e.g., between blue lines), for 15 to 20 minutes.
4. Skate 15 laps around the rink using long strides (only four strides for the length of the ice). Skate at 3/4 speed around the corners. Skate easy and coast for 5 minutes. Do this for 20 to 30 minutes.

5. Combine the above exercises or create others similar in format. Perform them skating backward as well, and alternate the direction in which you skate around the rink.

Explosive (Anaerobic) Endurance

When a hockey player uses sudden, intense bursts of power and speed, the oxygen system alone is insufficient to fulfill the energy demands of the body. In these situations additional energy is supplied by the muscle cells themselves. Nutrients within the cells (stored glycogen) are converted into energy for work without the presence or need of oxygen. In this *anaerobic* process of energy production, waste products (lactic acid) are given off and accumulate in the muscle cells.

Although the anaerobic energy system is critical to explosive movement, it is not nearly as efficient as the aerobic system in producing large quantities of energy. In addition, the accumulation of lactic acid in the cells causes rapid fatigue and a decrease in coordination, speed, and skill.

The focus of anaerobic training is to improve the efficiency of the cellular energy system—its ability to remove waste products from the muscle cells and transport them back into the blood stream quickly, thereby reducing their concentration within the cells. Anaerobic training also develops the player's ability to perform explosive bursts with greater accumulations of waste products in the muscle cells before succumbing to fatigue. With proper training a player is better prepared to skate all-out for an entire shift and recover completely during brief rest periods on the bench.

Anaerobic training consists of performing short bursts of intense activity as well as slightly longer intense activity. In both cases the activity must be performed at 100% effort. The activity is then followed by a rest period of two to three times the duration of the activity, allowing the body to transfer waste products from the cells into the blood stream. Full recovery is essential for optimum performance.

Training in which workouts alternate specific periods of work with specific periods of rest are called interval workouts. Work/rest ratios vary according to the purpose of the specific workout (e.g., anaerobic endurance, power, or quickness), and also depending upon the time of year (workouts become more intense as the hockey season progresses). Interval workouts can be conducted on dry land as well as on the ice.

It is imperative that while training for anaerobic endurance the player use skating-specific motions that work skating-specific muscle groups. Dryland activities such as bicycling, skating on Rollerblades Training Skates, and working out on the Heiden Slideboard develop and improve anaerobic endurance while maintaining specificity of the skating motion and muscle groups.

The Heiden Slideboard (shown later in Figure 12.14) was made famous as a training device by Olympic speedskating champion Eric Heiden. It can be easily built and is an excellent device for power training (use short work intervals such as 20 seconds:60 seconds) as well as endurance training (use longer work intervals such as 40 seconds:80 seconds). It is also excellent for practicing, away from the ice, the motions of the forward skating stride (technique development).

Exercises for Improving Anaerobic Endurance

Off-Ice Exercise

Sprint for 100 meters and then walk or jog slowly to rest, resting two to three times as long as it took to sprint. Do the same for 200, 300, and 400 meters.

On-Ice Exercise

Train with short, explosive sprints of 5 to 15 seconds followed by slow skating; also do longer sprints of up to 45 seconds followed by a rest period allowing for total recovery, using a work/rest ratio of 1:2 (sometimes a work/rest ratio of 1:3 is called for). Also, alternate skating at 100% effort for 15 seconds, easy for 45 seconds; at 100% effort for 30 seconds, easy for 90 seconds; at 100% effort for 45 seconds, easy for 90 seconds; at 75% effort for 45 seconds, easy for 90 seconds; and at 100% effort for 15 seconds, easy for 45 seconds.

Guidelines for On-Ice Endurance Training Intervals

When training for aerobic endurance, pro or college-age players should use intervals with a work ratio of 2:1—skate for 60 seconds, rest for 30 seconds. Skate at 3/4 speed during each work phase.

When training for anaerobic endurance, players should skate with maximum effort, using a work/rest ratio of 1:2—skate all out for 40 seconds, rest for 80 seconds. However, when doing stops and starts, a work/rest ratio of 1:3 is appropriate—work for 30 seconds, rest for 90 seconds.

Skill development, not endurance, is the top priority on ice for young skaters under age 16. Avoid on-ice drills specifically designed for endurance; as fatigue sets in, developing players often resort to poor skating techniques and the habits may become difficult to change. Control fatigue by using aerobic interval training.

Endurance for developing players is gained by the following:

1. Off-ice activities such as soccer, bicycling, running, and basketball. Some workouts should be aerobic, to build the all important aerobic base; others should be anaerobic. Off-ice activities do not interfere with skating skill, so these activities offer the most productive opportunity for endurance training.
2. The sum of all on-ice practice drills (60- to 90-minute sessions).
3. On-ice sprints at practice tempo. Keep work periods short enough so that fatigue does not destroy technique or skill development.

Training for Strength

To develop strength for its own sake is not an appropriate goal for hockey players. Their ultimate goal in building strength lies in the ability to apply that strength explosively. When strength is applied explosively, power results. Power, when combined with rapid leg motion, results in speed. Strength is, of course, a critical component of both power and speed and so must be developed.

Strong, flexible muscles are essential not only for power and speed but also for minimizing injury to soft tissues and joints. Players must train to strengthen the *specific* muscle groups used in hockey—those of the lower body used for skating (to develop greater speed), and those of the upper body used for shooting, checking, and withstanding body blows.

Strength training is the process of building muscle mass and recruiting more of the existing muscle fibers for work. Muscle mass can be gained from a variety of workouts that involve working against heavy resistance at various speeds (e.g., weight lifting at slow speeds). Muscle fiber recruitment is improved by intense lifting at specific speeds.

Strength training requires that the muscles to be strengthened be progressively overloaded. Adhering to this "overload principle" is critical; muscles, after being repeatedly forced to work beyond their present capability, eventually adapt to the new work level and perform effectively. At this point they must be overloaded again to develop an even greater capability for work. As long as the overload principle is followed, a variety of training methods can be used to achieve the same results; all require the muscles to work against resistance. Calisthenics, isometric training, partner resistance, and weight training are acceptable methods of increasing strength. Strength training should not be emphasized for youngsters. Wait until players are about 16 years old before stressing strength programs that rely on working against heavy resistance or weights.

Overloading is achieved in a number of ways: increasing the load to be moved (i.e., resistance or weight); increasing the length of each training session, the number of training sessions, or the number of repetitions per exercise; or increasing the load to be moved as well as increasing the number of repetitions and/or the number of sets of each exercise. Strength training takes place mostly off-ice.

The muscles of the lower body to be strengthened for skating are those of the hips, gluteals, adductors (groin), abductors (outer thighs), quadriceps, hamstrings, gastrocnemius (calves), and those of the feet and ankles.

The muscles of the upper body to be strengthened are those of the abdominals, back, chest, shoulders, arms, and neck. Keep in mind that the muscles of the upper body are used for skating as well as for shooting, checking, etc. For example, the back is used to control excessive upper body movement, the chest and arms are used to create correct and powerful arm swing, and the abdominals are used during each push. In all strength training it is important to train the muscles on both sides of the joint to maintain stability.

Calisthenics

These exercises use body weight as the resistance to be moved. Calisthenic exercises valuable for hockey players include push-ups, sit-ups, leg lifts, trunk raises, side and hip raises, wall squats, and chinning, as well as many others.

Isometric Training

Isometric training involves balanced and opposing equal forces of two or more complementary muscle groups. You may use arms to oppose legs, use arms and legs to oppose the central torso, use a given muscle group to oppose a fixed surface, or just power-flex one group of muscles (such as abdominal) until sufficient overload is achieved. Isometrics are especially useful when expensive weight-training equipment is not readily available.

Here is a sample isometric exercise: Lie on the floor, legs stretched in front of you, one on either side of a straight-legged chair. Press your legs inward against the chair. This simple exercise strengthens the adductor (groin) muscles.

Partner Resistance

This technique makes use of the overload principle as you move (i.e., skate) while pulling against a partner who is resisting the movement. All skating moves can be practiced against partner resistance.

Weight Training

Muscles are overloaded by the use of progressively heavier weights (dumbbells, barbells, machines, etc.). Begin training with light weights. Gradually increase the weight to be moved. Vary workouts from session to session so that different muscle groups are stressed. Weight training for strength development ultimately requires heavy loads. Learn to lift correctly to avoid injury. Programs should be designed for each individual and supervised by knowledgeable instructors.

Remember: Strength-training exercises tighten muscles. Warm up, stretch, and cool down gradually before and after each strength-training session.

Training for Power

Power is strength applied explosively. Power accompanied by rapid leg motion results in speed. Strength is not converted into power unless it is exerted explosively. One way to conceptualize the expression of power is to compare the muscles to the pistons in an automobile engine. The power stroke of an engine occurs when the compressed fuel-air mixture is exploded by a spark; the force of the explosion drives the piston and thus powers the automobile. Once strength is developed, one must train to develop powerful, quick legs, and then apply the power and quickness in the correct skating motion. Watch Mark Messier skate and you will see a demonstration of power converted into speed.

Power training, like strength training, involves progressively overloading *specific* muscle groups, but to train for power, increasing speed of motion (explosiveness) while working against resistance is essential. *Power skating* requires that the muscles specific to skating work explosively in the same range of motion as in skating and at the same speed (or even faster) as required by the sport of hockey (Blatherwick, 1986).

Power training workouts should be structured so that the athlete progressively increases the number of repetitions of each set of exercises while decreasing the time needed to work through each set. It is important for the athlete to continue working at speed even when fatigued, the purpose being to get beyond that threshold of fatigue and reach a new tolerance. (Note, however, that after a certain point increasing the number of sets or the number of repetitions in each set improves endurance but not power.)

A good general rule for power training with weights is to lift (or push or pull) 50% to 60% of your maximum weight capability for five sets of each exercise, with five repetitions in each set. Training with maximum loads will increase strength, but the speed will necessarily be slow, so power cannot be maximized; training with loads too light will produce very fast movement but the force will be too low to develop power. Each lift should be done with as much speed as possible, attempting to accelerate to the *end* of the range of motion on every lift. Acceleration and intensity are key factors. Squat jumps wearing a weighted vest or belt exemplify the effort to accelerate throughout the full range of motion. Work/rest ratios of power workouts must include a long enough rest period between sets or exercises so that each set can be performed explosively and with speed. If speed is slow, power will be low (Blatherwick, 1986).

The response to power training is fatigue. Recovery time is essential in order for the system to rest, rebuild, and adapt to a new level of work capability and fatigue tolerance. Muscle rebuilding time after power workouts is up to 48 hours, so power training workouts should be scheduled at least two days apart. Other types of workouts can be done in between.

Power-Training Workouts

As in endurance training, most (but not all) power training should take place off-ice so as not to interfere with quality skating. As with strength training, power training that relies on relatively heavy resistance is not recommended for skaters under 16 years of age.

Off-Ice Workouts.   Running uphill, interval running, working on the Heiden Slideboard, riding a bicycle uphill, riding a stationary bike (using interval workouts), using inner tubes from bicycles to provide resistance, calisthenics and partner resistance (all using submaximal resistance), and plyometric exercises (movement involving a recoil-spring principle) are all valid methods of power training on dry land. Rollerblades Training Skates are also a means of power training, using the leg muscles in skating-specific ways (Figures 12.10a and b). When using Rollerblades for power development, skate uphill. Coast down if the hill is slight or walk down if the hill is steep. Power training on Rollerblades has a distinct advantage: Since the legs move in the same manner and through the same range of motion as in skating, the skater can simultaneously practice skating technique.

On-Ice Workouts. On-ice power training is essential to perfect power skating development. Skating explosively against resistance is an essential aspect of power training on ice. Wearing a weight vest or weight belt, skating against partner resistance, or doing plyometric skating exercises are all valid means of accomplishing the same thing. However, muscles should not be overloaded too much. The resulting fatigue will affect the quality of skating as the fatigued skater resorts to poor skating techniques. Bad skating habits, often difficult to correct, may result (Blatherwick, 1986).

Use power intervals to develop powerful leg drive, moving the legs rapidly. Use a work/rest ratio of 1:5. For example, skate for 10 seconds, rest for 50 seconds; skate for 20 seconds, rest for 100 seconds. Wear weighted vests or belts with 50 to 60% of the maximum weight moved in strength training (this only for players 16 years or older).

Plyometrics

One of the most effective means of training for power is the technique called plyometrics (recoil bounding). Plyometrics links strength and sprint speed (Blatherwick, 1986). Plyometric exercises involve a quick recoil preceding an explosive spring; a coil-uncoil, stretch-contract action of the muscles. Examples are bounding, hopping, broad jumping, squat-jumps, leaping laterally over an obstacle, and jumping up stairs, all of which require great spring and agility.

Plyometric training is hard on the joints. It is important to establish flexibility and strength around the joints before participating in strenuous plyometric workouts.

Plyometric training works as follows:

1. Recoiling acts as a wind-up. The muscles, during the recoil, are stretched. Stretched muscles and tissues store energy like a rubber band. That stored energy becomes available for use upon muscle contraction.
2. When muscles are stretched quickly, they contract actively in a reflex interaction with nerves. This quick stretch/contract interactive pattern makes it possible to recruit muscle fibers in a more powerful manner (Blatherwick, 1986).

Plyometric Exercises

All plyometric exercises require a deep knee bend, a spring into the air, then another deep knee bend upon landing. This spring-bounding sequence is inherent to plyometric exercises.

Off-Ice Exercises

Step-Up, Step-Down

Step up onto a low bench (about 15 to 18 inches high) with your right foot and then with your left foot, so that both feet are on the bench. Then step back down with your right foot, then your left foot, so that both feet are on the floor. Keep repeating rapidly. Do the same exercise stepping up with your left foot and down with your right foot.

Standing Broad Jumps

Standing broad jumps are one of the most effective plyometric maneuvers, and are also an excellent means of practicing forward starts on dry land.

Perform continuous standing broad jumps on flat land and on slight inclines. Do 5 to 30 in a row. Concentrate on the coil/spring principle and on achieving as much forward distance as possible (see Figures 12.11a, b, and c).

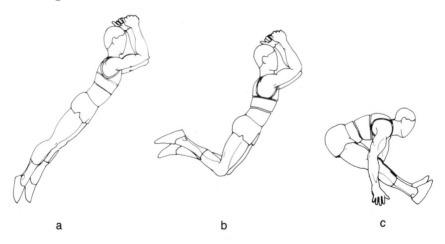

a   b   c

Figure 12.11 Standing broad jumps.

Jumps and Hops

See chapter 3 for instructions for these exercises. Both can be done on dry land or on ice.

On-Ice Exercises

Inside Edge Jumps

Set up an imaginary axis, or line, running the length of the ice and approximately 20 feet from the sideboards on your right. Skate forward, then glide on the RFI, aiming the glide directly away from the axis. Maintain a strong edge and knee bend as you glide. Skate a counterclockwise semi-circle. When you have curved a full 180 degrees, jump from the right foot as high off the ice as possible and land on the LFI. Land with a strong inside edge and knee bend of the left leg. Maintaining the edge and knee bend, glide on the LFI, aiming the glide directly away from the axis and skate a clockwise semi-circle. When you have curved a full 180 degrees jump from the left foot as high off the ice as possible and land on the RFI with a strong edge and knee bend of the right leg. You have completed one cycle. Keep repeating until you have completed one length of the ice. Keep your back straight, head up, and free foot off the ice and close to the skating foot throughout the exercise (Figure 12.12).

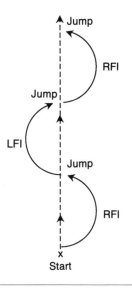

Figure 12.12   Inside edge jumps.

Variations:

1. Perform Inside Edge Jumps, but instead skate on, jump from, and land on outside edges.
2. Perform Inside and Outside Edge Jumps skating backward.

S Jumps

Refer to the S Curves exercise, chapter 7.

Remember: In this exercise you skate on the same foot throughout. Perform the exercise, but when changing from outside edge (RFO) to inside edge (RFI) or inside edge (RFI) to outside edge (RFO), jump off the ice to accomplish the change of edge. Jump as high off the ice as possible and land on a strong edge and deep knee bend of the landing leg. Keep the free foot off the ice and hold it close to the skating foot. See how many S jumps you can perform before putting the free foot on the ice. Keep your back straight and your head up throughout the exercise.

Repeat the exercise on your left foot. Then perform the exercise skating backward.

Training for Quickness

Quickness means fast feet, rapid leg motion. It is one of the most important qualities a hockey player can possess, for it vitally influences the ability to "rev up" and go. Watch Wayne Gretzky or Glen Anderson take off and you will know what quickness is and why it is so important.

Quickness is enhanced by a combination of factors, including proper skating technique, power, and rapid leg motion.

The purpose of hockey training and conditioning programs is to develop explosiveness and quickness. By incorporating these qualities with correct skating technique, speed, acceleration, and agility are improved. Quickness training aims to improve leg speed while still working the legs through their full range of motion. Until recently it was assumed that quickness is an innate quality. Now we know that quickness can be improved with dryland and on-ice training.

The younger you begin training for quickness, the greater the potential for its development. As players get older they must continue to train for quickness or this quality diminishes, just as flexibility, strength, power, and endurance diminish if they are not continuously trained.

Quickness training requires skating at top speed in all-out, explosive workouts. The bursts are intense and of short duration. Intervals using no resistance are the mode. Since quickness training forces players into an anaerobic state, long rest periods that allow for full recovery from fatigue are essential for the athlete to perform each repetition optimally.

The principles for achieving explosive acceleration and sprint speed in skating are virtually identical to those in running. The technical differences between the two lie in the differences in the surfaces pushed against; these require that the pushes be executed differently. Figure 12.13 shows the similarities between explosive skating starts and explosive running starts.

a   b

Figure 12.13   Explosive starts: skating and running.

Quickness Training Workouts

The purpose of quickness training workouts is to develop fast feet and sprint speed. They are executed at top speed and are nontechnical in nature. Since the intensity of quickness training can destroy skating technique, training for quickness on dry land is very effective. Workouts require total concentration and maximum effort. Players must be fresh and completely warmed up. Never do quickness workouts when players are fatigued or following strength or power workouts.

Workouts involve no resistance (to facilitate rapid movement) and can be performed daily with alternating workout intensities, performing light workouts one day and heavy the next. Movement must be fast paced. Slow movement only trains slowness.

Quickness training is *not* geared to conditioning, although improved conditioning is a by-product. Because of their weight, Rollerblades are not recommended for quickness training.

Work intervals should be short, rest intervals longer. A work/rest ratio of 1:5 or 1:10 allows for total recovery, which is necessary for each repetition to be performed with full intensity and optimum effort. For example, sprint for 10 seconds, rest for 50 seconds; sprint for 5 seconds, rest for 40 seconds; sprint for 8 seconds, rest for 40 to 80 seconds. The same applies for skating sprints.

Off-Ice Workouts

Sprint biking, sprint running (e.g., 30-meter dash) and slight downhill sprints are some of the means of quickness training on dry land.

Workouts for developing overall speed include running a 30-meter dash, a 60-meter dash, and/or a 100-meter dash. Leave enough time between sprints for complete recovery.

Explosive starts can be practiced on a track, on sand, or on grass. Explosiveness on the first five steps is of primary importance. To work on starts, run 20-meter sprints, running from a complete stop, and starting both forward and sideways. Standing broad jumps (Figure 12.11) help develop the forward "falling" feeling experienced in explosive starts. (Racing dives in a pool simulate the same feeling.)

Variations of quickness training on dry land are many:

- Sprint 20 meters, cut sharply to the side, sprint again, cut sharply to the other side.
- Incorporate crossovers, lateral leaps side to side and crossing over, sprints up and down slight inclines, and/or running backward. Do different combinations of the above at top (even out-of-control) speeds.
- Another aspect of quickness is BAM: balance, agility, and maneuverability. Coordination and flexibility exercises such as tumbling, rolling, jumping, hopping, juggling, gymnastic moves, dribbling balls with the feet, running obstacle courses, or performing moves with no previous knowledge of the move to be demanded, all while moving fast, are good ways to improve quickness and BAM.

Remember: Quality, intensity, and top speed are essential. When tired and quality is suffering, or when you're not accomplishing anything, switch to another kind of workout. And, if muscles are sore, delay speed work until the soreness is gone.

On-Ice Workouts

The goal on-ice is to develop the fastest possible leg rhythm while moving the legs correctly, powerfully, and through their full range of motion. Since skill and quickness on ice are developed while skating, on-ice skating drills should be geared toward skill and speed development rather than endurance development. Once correct skating techniques are established, on-ice sprint intervals may be the most important aspect of a player's training program. With or without the puck, the point is to perform everything at *top speed*. In game situations and even in practices players rarely skate as fast as they would if they were being timed. Players slow down to carry the puck, to receive a pass, to wait for the play, etc. In practices they inadvertently slow down, fearing a fall or loss of the puck in front of their coach or teammates.

The neuromuscular system can be thought of as a computer: It records (for future performance) everything you do, whether fast or slow, correct or incorrect. If you practice skating technique only at slow speeds you will teach yourself slowness. You *must* learn to skate correctly, then to skate correctly *fast* (Blatherwick, 1986). Therefore, when training for quickness on the ice, practice all the skating maneuvers discussed in this book at out-of-control speeds. Remember: These sessions are nontechnical in nature. It is better to fall or lose the puck during quickness intervals than to slow down just to be in control or to avoid mistakes. In fact, players should push themselves to speeds which *cause* mistakes. This must be repeated until players become comfortable at the new speed. Then they must go beyond that speed, to a new out-of-control speed, again making mistakes as they learn, until they are comfortable at that new level of speed. When combined with slower exercises to learn and improve technique, these sprints develop higher levels of ability to perform top speed maneuvers in control. Strive for progressively greater speed, increased quickness, more agility, and the three Cs— control, composure, and comfort. When you achieve the three Cs you will have attained the ability to perform quality maneuvers at top speed in game situations (Wenger, 1986).

The sprint exercises described for quickness training on dry land can also be done on ice. Keep the on-ice sprints short (from 20 to 100 meters), leaving time for full recovery between repetitions. Other dryland exercises can be used on-ice as well: tumbling, jumping, hopping, juggling, dribbling pucks with the feet, skating obstacle courses, and performing a variety of skating moves with no previous knowledge of the moves to be done. All moves must be performed while skating fast.

Mental Quickness

Another aspect of quickness training is mental quickness, or mental preparedness. The ability to anticipate, make quick decisions, and respond instantly to changing conditions can be learned and enhanced by awareness training. Players who learn to know where others are and what others are doing while they themselves are performing intricate maneuvers at great speed are the ones who anticipate, read plays, react, and move quickly in games.

Train yourself to be aware of your teammates and your opponents as much of the time as possible. This awareness can be increased considerably by developing your peripheral vision. Practice by focusing on a point directly in front of you and thinking about what you see out of the corners of your eyes. Mentally list the things you see. Practice determining color and spotting movement at the corners of your vision. Have someone hold up various colored objects off to one side and then the other. Keep your eyes focused straight ahead as your partner brings the objects slowly into your field of vision from behind you and off to the sides. Call out "now" followed by the color as soon as you can see the movement. With practice you can more quickly spot pucks, sticks, and players and also determine the colors of jerseys.

Dryland Training for Skating Technique

Until recently, training for ice hockey skating technique has been confined almost exclusively to on-ice situations. We have made little use of dry land to develop and practice skating technique. However, with ice time as precious as it is, and with the overwhelming amount of skill work which must be covered in limited practice sessions, it has become increasingly important to use dry land to develop and practice correct skating movement.

Dryland skating, used for technique training, offers the following advantages:

1. Skaters can practice the exact motions and body positions of the skating strides (forward, backward, crossovers, starts, etc.) in a slow, exaggerated manner.
2. Coaches can give instruction, have discussions, and answer questions away from the ice, freeing ice time for implementing and actual practice of the skating moves.
3. Already discussed are the applications of Rollerblades Training Skates and the Heiden Slideboard for simulating the skating strides and practicing skating technique. Figure 12.14 illustrates the use of the Heiden Slideboard.

Dryland skating, when used to develop and practice correct skating techniques, should initially be conducted at low levels of speed and resistance so players can *Feel, Act, See* and *Think* (FAST) about

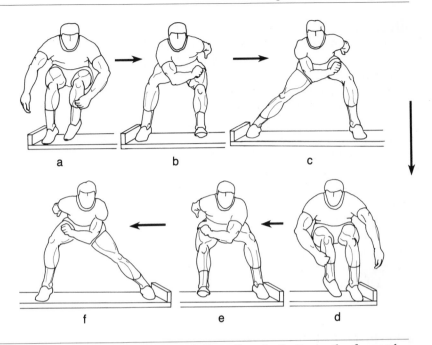

a   b   c

f   e   d

Figure 12.14   Heiden Slideboard: Note the similarity to the forward skating stride.

executing each segment of the skating move being worked on. In the learning stages each movement should be exaggerated, and each stride and position executed as perfectly as possible. Technique and fitness should *not* be trained together—there is a time to concentrate on developing correct technique just as there is a time to concentrate on conditioning (Holum, 1984). Remember: Fatigue destroys technique! As the correct motions and body positions become ingrained, the speed of execution should be gradually increased until each skating maneuver can be performed correctly at top speed.

Some dryland exercises that can be used to practice skating technique are shown in Figures 12.15 through 12.19.

When performing dryland skating exercises apply the principles of body weight, knee bend, and the correct push and recovery of the specific skating stride being practiced.

Maintaining the Level of Conditioning

When involved in a heavy schedule of competition it is impossible to continue a rigid conditioning program. To hold the training effect at a high level but avoid the fatigue that accompanies heavy

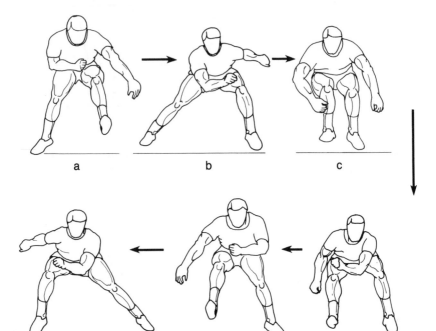

Figure 12.15   Lateral skating: Make skating motions from side to side rather than forward; note knee bend of support leg.

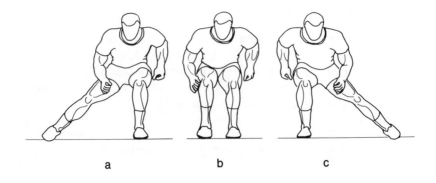

Figure 12.16   Side steps: Push to side, return feet together, using the opposite leg to push each time; maintain deep knee bend as the leg returns.

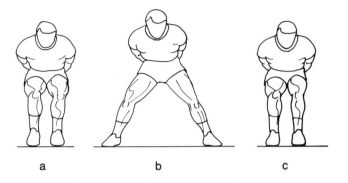

Figure 12.17 In-and-out jumps: Jump out in split-like position; return legs under body, maintaining knee bend as legs return.

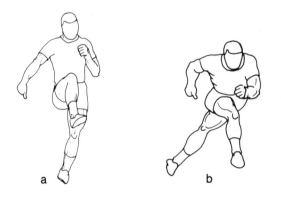

Figure 12.18 Crossovers: Practice crossover/crossunder moves; note full extension of pushing leg under the body.

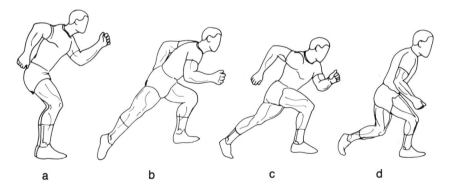

Figure 12.19 Sprint starts: Practice sprint starts on a track, starting both from a frontal and side position.

training, hockey players should go on a maintenance program during these times. Decrease the duration of training sessions but keep the intensity high. Also, decrease the number of workouts to once or twice a week, as scheduling allows.

At all times it is important to get enough rest, follow a quality diet, and drink *lots* of water when skating, playing, and working out.

Other Sports

Hockey is hard work—it is important to relax and take a break once in a while. During the off season, other sporting activities provide variety and are excellent supplements to hockey-specific training. Sports that involve running (basketball, soccer, track, etc.) use the leg muscles in different motions than skating but develop overall quickness, coordination, agility, and endurance. Sports such as rowing, swimming, and wrestling develop and improve upper body strength and power. Jumping rope (on a cushioned surface) and lateral and backward running and dancing (especially ballet) are excellent for balance, coordination, and agility. Cycling (on the road and on a stationary bike) and use of a nordic track machine are excellent workouts for the quadriceps.

Summary

Follow these guidelines for safe and effective conditioning and training:

- Use proper warm-up, cool-down, and flexibility activities and exercises before and after workouts.
- Use a combination of on-ice and dryland training methods to improve skating: Always overload for strength and power; underload for quickness and agility; and vary work/rest ratios and intensities in interval work to develop aerobic and anaerobic endurance. On the ice, combine correct skating technique with power, quickness, and agility—the formula for speed.

Sprint intervals on-ice are essential for developing the ability to apply power in a rapid skating motion.

Quality skating drills combining speed work with technique work are the most important ingredients of training for hockey.

Repetition guarantees that learning will be permanent. But only *correct* repetition guarantees that learning will be *correct* and permanent. Practice correctly!

REFERENCES
AND RECOMMENDED READINGS

Alter, J. (1983). *Surviving exercise: Judy Alter's safe and sane exercise book*. Boston: Houghton Mifflin.

Blatherwick, J. (1986). *Team U.S.A. year round training*. Colorado Springs, CO: Amateur Hockey Association of the United States.

Endestad, A., and Teaford, J. (1987). *Skating for cross-country skiers*. Champaign, IL: Leisure Press.

Holum, D. (1984). *The complete handbook of speed skating*. Hillside, NJ: Enslow.

Radcliffe, J., and Farentinos, R. (1985). *Plyometrics*. Champaign, IL: Human Kinetics.

Wenger, H. (1986). *Fitness: The key to hockey success*. Victoria, BC: British Columbia Amateur Hockey Association.

GLOSSARY

Abductor muscles—The muscles of the outer thigh, used to push the leg away from the center of the body.

Adductor muscles—The muscles of the inner thigh and groin, used to draw the leg inward toward the center of the body.

Aerobic—In the presence of oxygen.

Anaerobic—In the absence of oxygen.

Ball of the foot—The metatarsal area of the foot, immediately behind the toes.

Center of gravity—That segment or part of the body under which the feet must be situated in order to maintain balance.

Centrifugal force—The force that impels a body outward from the center of rotation.

Centripetal force—The force that impels a body inward toward the center of rotation.

Counter—The reinforced arch support of the skates.

Crossover—The two-step sequence used to maneuver and gain speed on a curve. The inside skate glides on the outside edge of the blade as the outside leg thrusts from the inside edge. After the thrust, the outside skate crosses over in front of the inside skate and takes the ice on its inside edge. Simultaneously, the inside leg drives sideways under the body toward the outside of the curve as it thrusts against the outside edge of the blade.

Deke—To fake.

Edge of the blade—The sharp part of each skate blade that cuts into the ice. There are two edges on each blade. The following abbreviations are used throughout the book to describe the edges used to perform skating maneuvers:

- **RFI**—Right foot skating forward on the inside edge
- **RFO**—Right foot skating forward on the outside edge
- **RBI**—Right foot skating backward on the inside edge
- **RBO**—Right foot skating backward on the outside edge
- **LFI**—Left foot skating forward on the inside edge
- **LFO**—Left foot skating forward on the outside edge
- **LBI**—Left foot skating backward on the inside edge
- **LBO**—Left foot skating backward on the outside edge

Flat of the blade—Both edges engaged on the ice simultaneously. The glide will be straight ahead.

Flexibility—The ability to move a muscle group through its full range of motion.

Free foot, hip, leg, shoulder, or side—Those parts of the body that correspond to the skate that is off the ice.

Full extension—The part of the stride where the knee of the gliding leg is well bent and the thrusting leg is locked and as far away from the body as it will stretch.

Gastrocnemius—The muscle in the back of the calf.

Gliding foot (skate)—The foot on which the full body weight is sustained while moving over the ice. Also known as the skating foot.

Gluteal muscles—The muscles of the buttocks.

Groin—The crease at the junction of the thigh with the trunk.

Groin muscles—Muscles of the groin area.

Hamstring muscles—The long muscles in the back of the upper leg.

Inside edges of the blades—The blade edges closer to the insides of the boots.

Inside foot (skate)—When one is skating a curve, the foot (skate) closer to the center of the circle or curve.

Inside shoulder—When one is skating a curve, the shoulder closer to the center of the curve.

Lower body—The body from the hips down: hips, buttocks, legs, and feet.

Mohawk turn—A two-step maneuver that turns the skater from forward to backward or backward to forward, involving a change of feet during the turn.

Outside edges of the blades—The blade edges closer to the outsides of the boots.

Outside foot (skate)—When one is skating a curve, the foot (skate) closer to the outside of the curve.

Outside shoulder—When one is skating a curve, the shoulder closer to the outside of the curve.

Plyometrics—Movements or exercises involving recoil-bounding (coil-spring) actions.

Quadriceps (Thigh muscles)—The muscles at the front of the upper leg.

Rock of the skate blade—The convex curvature of the blade.

Skating foot, hip, leg, shoulder, side—Those parts of the body that correspond to the skate that is engaged on the ice.

Thrusting foot (pushing foot)—The foot that pushes against the ice to propel the skater.

Toe of the blade—The extreme front of the inside or outside edge of the blade, including the curved portion, which provides the final push.

Torque—A turning or twisting force.

Traveling on a curve or circle—Moving in a clockwise or counterclockwise direction.

Turn—Changing from skating forward to skating backward, or from backward to forward.

Upper body—The parts of the body from the waist up: waist, abdomen, chest, back, arms, shoulders, and head.

ABOUT THE AUTHOR

Laura Stamm and Keith Gretzky

Laura Stamm, the first woman ever to have coached a major league professional hockey team, has shown the hockey world how important skating technique is to a player's success. Her love for skating and hockey along with her training in sports, science, and teaching have led to her acknowledged reputation as a master teacher of hockey skating.

A champion athlete in ice dancing and tennis, Laura majored in physiology at Cornell University and went on to teach high school biology and physics. In 1971 she became a power skating coach at a summer hockey school directed by then–NHL stars Rod Gilbert and Brad Park. She then went on to coach rookie New York Islander star Bob Nystrom. Her enormous success with him led to coaching assignments with other teams in the NHL and WHA (World Hockey Association); she has taught hundreds of pro players how to increase their speed, ability, and efficiency on the ice. Some of Laura's young

NHL stars have included Luc Robitaille, Kevin Dineen, Doug Brown, Kelly Hrudey, and Scott Young.

Laura, along with her certified coaching associates, currently conducts power skating clinics for players from peewee to pro throughout the United States and Canada. She is the director of power skating for the Okanagan Hockey Schools in Western Canada and is a noted speaker and TV personality. Her previous books and videos on power skating have established the standard for power skating instruction.

Laura's other interests include tennis, dancing, backpacking, photography, and music. She and her sons Jeffrey and Richard live in the New York City area.